Plate 1.

COLORADO

Off Diamond Head, Oahu, 1926

The *Colorado*-class battleships were the first to be laid down under the major U.S. naval expansion program authorized in 1916. They mounted twin 16" guns in their four superimposed centerline turrets. This classic layout was early favored by the U.S. Navy, because no guns are located amidships with restricted fields of fire.

After U.S entry to the war in 1917, battleship construction was suspended in favor of more urgently needed anti-submarine craft and merchant shipping. Only three of the *Colorado* class were completed.

The dawn view of the splendid battleship *Colorado* leading the Pacific Fleet away from Pearl Harbor shows a number of interesting details. There are range clocks immediately below the big two-story spotting tops on her cage masts and bearing indicators painted on Number 2 turret. These features were adopted after it had been found at Jutland how difficult it was to judge the range and bearing at which other ships in the line were directing their fire. *Colorado* has two aircraft

catapults, one on Number 3 turret, and she carries Vought 02 Corsair float planes for gunnery spotting.

The battleship is flying the international code flag for "Undergoing a speed trial." Ships would normally carry out full-power trials at intervals of roughly six months.

Plate 2.

CAESAR

Grand Harbour, Malta, 1899

The battleship *Caesar* approaches her moorings in Grand Harbour in a setting that has little changed to this day.

Decks are spotless from daily scrubbing with holystone; teak and brasswork glitter in the sun; and canvas awnings, taut and immaculate, shade the quarterdeck and Admiral's stern-walk. A white-helmeted Marine band plays as the battleship proceeds splendidly up the harbor with the Vice-Admiral's flag snapping from her foremast. Nothing could equal the swank of the Mediterranean Fleet.

On the extreme left is Fort St. Angelo, stronghold of La Valette, Grand Master of the Knights of St. John during the Great Siege. The fortifications were largely built to the design of Italian engineers during the years following the Turkish assault of 1565.

The small craft in the foreground are *dghaisas*, a Maltese specialty and near-cousin of the Venetian gondola.

Caesar, a typical pre-Dreadnought, was one of nine ships of the *Majestic* class completed from 1895-98. *Majestic*-class ships mounted the new high-velocity Armstrong wire-wound 12" gun using "smokeless powder" (cordite propellant). Their 6" guns were quick firers, with integral cartridge and shell, and the ships were the first to be equipped with telescopic sights.

Plate 3.
MIKASA
Newcastle-upon-Tyne, 1902

The Armstrong shipyard at Elswick was situated upriver from Newcastle-upon-Tyne. The city center lies some eight miles from the river mouth at a point where the Tyne flows between high ground on both sides; the older part of the city is built on a hillside that drops steeply to the water.

It was a proud day when warships built at Elswick were eased downriver at low tide to give maximum clearance as they passed under the High Level Bridge; hundreds of spectators turned out to watch and cheer.

Not the last battleship to make the passage, the Japanese *Mikasa* was undoubtedly the most famous. She survived Russian guns off Port Arthur and served as Admiral Togo's flagship at the Battle of the Yellow Sea and at Tsushima. Today she is still afloat, maintained in honor as a national monument at Yokosuka.

Mikasa was one of the first ships to be protected by armor cemented by the Krupp process. This involved heating the plates to a great temperature before quenching them in oil to harden the face while maintaining a degree of elasticity. The material, a chrome-nickel-steel alloy, gave 20-percent better resistance than face-hardened Harvey steel.

Note the Admiral's stern walk wrapped around the rear end of the ship. The peacetime color scheme resembles that of a smart passenger liner; in 1904 the Japanese ships were painted grey.

Plate 4.

RODNEY

Portsmouth, England, 1944

Rodney and her sister ship *Nelson*, built from 1922 to 1927, featured a design restricted in size by the terms of the Washington Treaty. They followed the precedent set by Japanese and American battleships in mounting 16"-caliber guns, which were concentrated in three triple turrets forward, thereby reducing the extent of the necessary armor protection to magazines.

The original design called for a displacement of 50,000 tons and a speed of 32 knots, but in order to reduce the displacement to 34,000 tons, sacrifices were made, including cutting the ships' speed down to 23 knots. The design incorporated many lessons from wartime experience, particularly the high freeboard with secondary armament mounted in turrets on the upper deck and a greatly improved scheme of protection derived from tests carried out on captured ships.

During the Second World War, *Rodney* played an important role in the sinking of the *Bismarck*. Her 16" guns scored a hit on the German battleship in the third salvo, which contributed to the rapid silencing of the powerful ship. *Rodney*'s foredeck was buckled and distorted by the blast from her own heavy guns. In the picture *Rodney* is just casting off from South Railway Jetty in Portsmouth Dockyard, with the masts of Nelson's *Victory* visible on the right. She is flying her recognition signal, "Battleship 24," and the familiar Blue Peter, "The vessel is about to put to sea. All personnel are to return aboard immediately."

Dedicated to His Excellency M. Christian de Saint Hubert,
Ambassador of Belgium to Brazil

Edited by Kathleen D. Valenzi.
Designed by Carolyn Weary Brandt.
Art direction by Marilyn F. Appleby.
Editorial assistance provided by Christopher D. Daly.
Paintings and text copyright © 1990 Ian Marshall. All rights reserved.

Library of Congress Catalog Card Number 90-81634
ISBN 0-943231-34-5

Printed and bound in Singapore by Tien Wah Press.

Published by Howell Press, Inc., 700 Harris Street, Suite B,
Charlottesville, VA 22901. Telephone (804) 977-4006.

First printing

HOWELL PRESS

ARMORED SHIPS

THE SHIPS, THEIR SETTINGS, AND THE ASCENDANCY THAT
THEY SUSTAINED FOR 80 YEARS.

PAINTINGS AND TEXT BY IAN MARSHALL

FOREWORD BY ADMIRAL SIR ANTHONY GRIFFIN, GCB

PREFACE

Purists will be aware that, strictly speaking, the term Armored Ship was confined to a warship with a vertical belt of armor plating along the sides of the hull in the neighborhood of the waterline. A ship whose protection consisted of no more than an armored deck (invariably not the weather deck but one close to the level of the waterline) was described as a protected cruiser. I have included both types, for ships like *Emden Königsberg*, which had only horizontal deck protection, are supremely representative of the era.

Changes took place in the appearance of every warship during her service life. I have tried to portray each ship as she was in the year of the caption. In many cases, however, the evidence is hard to find, and I will be grateful to anyone who can improve my knowledge. The same thing is true of the geographical settings.

My most heartfelt thanks go to my wife, whose boundless patience buoyed the enterprise and who committed every word to floppy disc. Thanks go to Lieutenant-Commander Peter Whitehead, R.N., and to Oliver Swann, whose enthusiasm and advice encouraged me to persevere. I am most grateful to my brother in Nairobi, who scrutinized the manuscript under a microscope for errors of fact, and to Admiral Sir Anthony Griffin GCB, R.N., for most generously consenting to write the foreword. Captain Chatterton Dickson, R.N., commander of the naval signal school, HMS *Mercury*, was extremely helpful on the knotty subject of signal flag codes.

I.H.M., Mount Desert Island, Maine, 1990

Plate 5.

MISSOURI
Villefranche, South of France, 1946

After the Second World War, it looked for a time as if much of Western Europe might be snatched into the Communist camp. It happened in Czechoslovakia, it very nearly happened in Greece and in Italy, and even in France democracy seemed to waver. In 1946, as part of an effort to strengthen the hand of elected governments, the battleship *Missouri*, in which the Japanese surrender had been signed in Tokyo Bay on September 2, 1945, was sent to Show the Flag in the Mediterranean.

In this picture "Mighty Mo" is observed from a belvedere in the neglected, overgrown garden of a villa at Villefranche, the deepwater anchorage near Nice on the French Riviera.

Once part of the Kingdom of Sardegna, Villefranche had been made available to the Russians in the 1860s as a coaling station for their Mediterranean Squadron. After the *Risorgimento* and the emergence of modern Italy, this area became part of France, and the right to use the naval facilities at Villefranche was transferred to the United States. During the 1870s American warships regularly called there, and subsequently it became, and remains, the principal port of call for foreign warships visiting the South of France.

Plate 6.

NEW MEXICO and TEXAS

Pedro Miguel Locks, Panama Canal, 1919

The Panama Canal was not opened to international traffic until 1920, but the new battleship *New Mexico* passed through the canal from Atlantic to Pacific soon after the end of the First World War. She is seen in one of the Pedro Miguel Locks, beginning her descent from Gatun Lake, which is 85 feet above sea level. She will pass through two more locks at Miraflores before reaching the Pacific.

The older battleship *Texas* is entering the other lock, in which the water level is still

the same as that of the lake; *New Mexico* is some 30 feet lower. An immense volume of water is discharged as ships climb or descend through the locks. The water is replenished from the great artificial lake that was created in the center of the isthmus. Fortunately the rainfall is one of the heaviest in the world.

Small electric locomotives called mules are used to maneuver ships into and out of the locks. A steam passenger train of the Panama Railroad can be seen on the right of the picture. Passengers have turned out to watch

the novelty of the battleships' passage.

Canvas awnings have been rigged to shade the decks of both ships in the torrid climate.

CONTENTS

PAINTINGS

PENCIL SKETCHES

Ian Marshall's paintings are exhibited at the Oliver Swann Galleries, 170 Walton Street, London SW3 2JL, England.

Plate 7.

MAINE

Casco Bay, 1897

Maine, the first battleship to join the U.S. Navy, is seen here lying in Casco Bay, Maine, two years after her commissioning. Note the way in which the port stern barbette carrying one of her pair of twin 10"-gun turrets overhangs the side of the ship. The turrets were disposed so that both could be brought to bear forward, astern, or on either broadside. There were gaps between the three islands of the superstructure to allow this, bridged over by walkways, but the field of fire across deck was severely restricted, and muzzle blast could cause damage to the superstructure.

The steam torpedo boat in the picture was one of a pair designed to be carried on board. The boats carried a single Whitehead torpedo in a bow tube, but they proved too slow and were soon discarded.

Maine suffered a disastrous explosion while visiting the Cuban port of Havana in 1898, causing the death of 260 out of her total crew of 370 men. It has never been determined for sure whether the cause of the tragedy was accidental or due to sabotage, but the sinking of the battleship triggered the start of the Spanish-American War.

by Admiral Sir Anthony Griffin GCB

True stories when sensitively written and beautifully illustrated present history in its most engaging form.

This book is no exception. It is a history of one of the most dramatic products of the Industrial Revolution, which, with its steam, iron, and machinery, led to armored ships and thence to further remodeling of world history.

These ships could move swiftly and surely, almost regardless of the weather, to wherever they were needed. There, armed with the most powerful weapons in the world, they could, over an indefinite period, exert pressure through a choice of goodwill, menace, or violence. Throughout most of the twentieth century, they could also be controlled by wireless.

Nations could thus project influence throughout the world's oceans and much of the land as well, since most people have always lived close to the sea and depended on seaborne trade for their survival.

Consequently, armored ships became a symbol of nationhood. This was further enhanced by an ability to design and build them, since those countries without such an ability ran the risk of their ships being seized before delivery if the building country needed them.

Ian Marshall has collected and presented all the best stories about armored ships and how they were conceived, built, and operated throughout the world. Some never fired a shot in anger. Others seemed never to be far from dramatic action or destruction in horrific battles in which their opponents were frequently not other armored ships but mines, submarines, or aircraft. It was these latter weapons that eventually drove the armored ship not off the seas but off its dominant position as one of the most powerful arbiters of world affairs.

As ever, the central feature of this history was the people—those with the vision to conceive, with the skill to design and build, and with the intelligence and courage to operate, fight, and often die with these unique creations.

Such a pattern was and is the stuff of progress. Success spelled not just survival but often prosperity too. The underlying human theme of this remarkable book, as exemplified through the armored ship, is of course universal.

INTRODUCTION

Starting in the year 1861 and ending in December 1941, the armored ship was arbiter of much of the world's affairs. Her presence at the scene of a confrontation could be a gesture: menacing, reassuring, or boastful. Lying at anchor off the palmy beach at Apia or stemming the swift current in the Bosporus, standing out to sea from the cliffs of Agadir or flaunting the flag up the Yangtze, escorting *Hohenzollern* to the Kaiser's summer palace on Corfu, or training the guns on the waterfront at Zanzibar, her presence was a token of resources that extended far beyond the horizon.

A little after the middle of the last century, the earliest armored warships began to appear at sea. Set against the smooth-bore muzzle-loading cannon of the day, such a ship was almost invulnerable, and it soon became apparent that the only means of stopping her was to put to sea a superior force of her own kind.

It was useless to confront a vessel like *Monitor* with even a whole squadron of wooden frigates. But between ships of the same category a slight edge in technology could prove decisive. A ship mounting guns of slightly greater range and penetrating power could outreach a superior force of the enemy, or a small advantage in speed could outweigh inferiority in numbers.

Nations with vital seaborne interests devoted, therefore, enormous resources to developing the best in armored ships. In contrast to warfare on land, where gigantic numbers of men and prolonged campaigns were needed to secure results, command of the sea might be gained in a single brief encounter. The outcome of a naval battle could be decided by some narrow but significant advantage in matériel, or lost, perhaps, by a trivial mechanical defect.

For 80 years the armored ship was Queen. She was never again as immune as in the first flush dawn of the 1860s, but she remained the ultimate weapon until the time came when torpedo-carrying aircraft became capable of stopping her dead in the water.

As late as 1944 the battleship *Tirpitz* lurking in her Norwegian fjord was perceived as a threat so serious and so difficult to stop by any other means that a superior force of battleships had constantly to be maintained at Scapa Flow in case she should emerge.

Undoubtedly the most stirring exploit was that of the German battle cruiser *Goeben* in August 1914. One ship, commanded with brilliant effrontery, brought about the commitment of Turkey to a war in which she had no resolve to join. The military consequences were inordinate, prolonging the Great War by at least a year, and the political changes that flowed from Turkish involvement were immeasurable.

The ships, of course, were not all. It took years to train crews to operate and men to command. A ship without her complement was a paper tiger.

Steamships, unlike their sailing forebears or nuclear-powered successors, were tied closely to shore bases for coaling and repair. For many years ships' engines were so uneconomical that range was severely restricted, and the use of untried technology

background of industrial capability, dockyards, and widespread coaling stations.

It was the long reach of sea power that made it so effective. A nation with slender resources had the power to intervene strategically, if it held command of the sea, and it could deny a far stronger adversary freedom of movement. In a book published in 1890, the American naval historian Captain Alfred Mahan articulated the policy that had been tacitly followed by Britain for 250 years. He concluded that "control of the sea is chief among the material elements in the power and prosperity of nations." Captain Mahan's concept of the Fleet in Being, a naval force held ready, poised for action but not committed, was the special asset of a maritime power.

Unless they put to sea, however, both ships and crews would inevitably decline. A fleet swinging idly at its moorings slowly lost the skills and the nerve that are called upon to fight successfully at sea.

In the 30 months of inaction following its rebuff at the Battle of Jutland, the German High Seas Fleet steadily decayed; the same happened to the Russians in Port Arthur in 1904 and to the Italians after the Battle of Cape Matapan in 1941. Germany was starved into submission by the Royal Navy's command of the sea in the First World War, and the one great collision between battle fleets never changed the status quo.

This book is an attempt to evoke, in pictures as well as in words, something of the era of the armored ship.

carried the handicap of unreliability. Often it was mechanical shortcomings that determined the fortunes of war.

The maintenance of sea power, therefore, required not only ships, the very latest and the very best, but it depended on thoroughly drilled and dedicated manpower, on constant evolutions at sea, and on a

Plate 8.

PHLEGETHON and **DIDO**

Batang Lupar River, Sarawak, 1843

The world's first iron warships were paddle steamers built for the Honourable East India Company in the 1830s. Two of them, *Nemesis* and *Phlegethon*, played a critical role in the Opium War in China 1841-43 and in the First Burma War 1852-53.

In 1843 *Phlegethon*, accompanied by the square-rigged corvette *Dido*, took part in an expedition to suppress piracy on the north coast of Borneo. This culminated in an assault, illustrated here, up one of the principal rivers of Sarawak.

No military force of the era could match the concentrated firepower of a European man-of-war. Paddle steamers towed the wooden square-rigged ships into action, but further up river the new iron warships carried the flag on their own. The powered vessels bore down inexorably on vessels under oar, and with their swivel-mounted, 32-pounder cannon and rocket launchers, they proved well capable of subduing forts on the river banks. The Indian Navy established command of the Red Sea, the Persian Gulf, the Irrawaddy, the Pearl River, and the Yangtze-Kiang. British naval power, restricted hitherto to the high seas where her wooden sailing ships were undisputed, was now capable of being projected by steam gunboats deep into the great land masses of southern and eastern Asia.

Phlegethon is flying the Company Jack, the gridiron flag of the Honourable East India Company, which carries the Union flag in the first canton.

Plate 9.

WARRIOR

Plymouth Sound, 1864

Warrior entered service in the Royal Navy in 1861. One of the very first armored ships, she was the first to be constructed of iron. She can be seen today in Portsmouth Dockyard, splendidly restored and open to the public.

Warrior is a large ship, 420 feet long, compared with 180 feet of Nelson's *Victory*. Her armor is 4½"-thick wrought iron over 18" of teak, and her hull is subdivided into water-tight compartments. For the first few years of her life, this protection was sufficient to resist any gunfire, and in theory she could sail the seas with complete impunity.

Warrior was built to catch and destroy the new French ironclads. Fourteen of her guns were big breech-loading rifles that could fire 110-pound shot or shell. Her remaining 26 guns were 68-pound cannon, twice the size of those in general use. Ten years would pass before anyone produced armor capable of resisting them.

Her engines could drive her at a healthy 14 knots, but *Warrior* once made 17.5 knots under sail and steam combined. She had a single screw, which could be retracted.

Contemporary ships-of-the-line carried three decks of guns, up to 120 cannon, and their towering wooden sides were painted with strakes (horizontal bands) of ocher or white between the black to emphasize the number of gunports. Lord Palmerston, contemplating the long black hull of the ironclad, described her as "a snake amongst the rabbits."

CHAPTER I

THE INNOVATORS:
WARRIOR, MONITOR,
HUASCAR AND DEVASTATION

The armored ship evolved as a result of three independent technological developments. First came steam power, introduced initially for paddle tugs in the early years of the nineteenth century. By the 1820s merchant ships with steam engines were making regular ocean voyages, and the first crossing of the Atlantic under steam was made in 1838. Engines and boilers were both inefficient and unreliable, so a ship's endurance under power was severely limited, and until the last quarter of the nineteenth century, engines were generally regarded as only an auxiliary source of propulsion.

Second came the use of iron for construction. The first really large ocean-going iron ship was I. K. Brunel's steamer *Great Britain*, completed at Bristol in 1843. The iron frigate *Princeton* was built for the U.S. Navy in the same year.

Third was the development of explosive shells. While traditional heavy-timber construction was remarkably resistant to solid shot fired from smooth-bore cannon at anything but the closest range, the new projectiles would create an inferno in a timber ship.

Explosive shells, incidentally, were also hazardous to those who used them. An accident on board *Princeton* in 1844 caused the deaths of not only the Secretary of the Navy but also the Secretary of State.

Early experiments showed that iron plating would shatter under the impact of solid shot, creating no less a hazard within an iron ship than the explosion of shells inside a timber one. But iron plating bolted to the outside of heavy timbers seemed to provide an effective protection. Right up until the 1920s, it was the practice to fix armor plating onto timber backing along the sides of a ship's hull.

During the Crimean War the French employed shallow-draft wooden "floating batteries" protected by iron plating. The commander of the Russian forts at Kinburn surrendered in despair when his cannon proved powerless against the attackers. France thereupon decided to embark on the construction of ocean-going ironclad warships.

To the resurgent France of Napoleon III the combination of iron cladding on ships armed with guns that fired explosive shells seemed to offer the prospect of creating a navy that would counterbalance Britain's preponderance in conventional wooden men-of-war. France's naval power had been shattered by the Royal Navy in the course of the Napoleonic Wars, and although the two countries found themselves allies on behalf of the Turks against Russia, by and large they were rivals throughout the nineteenth century.

The first of the new French warships, *La Gloire*, was completed in 1860. She had a belt of armor along the waterline consisting of 4.5"-thick wrought iron over a backing of 18" teak. Such protection was beyond the capacity of contemporary guns to penetrate.

The appearance of *La Gloire* caused considerable alarm in Britain, where experimental work on the performance of armor plating had been carried on at a much less enthusiastic pace.

Public opinion was aroused, even to wild talk of the threat of French invasion. British industrial capacity was mobilized, tenders were sought from

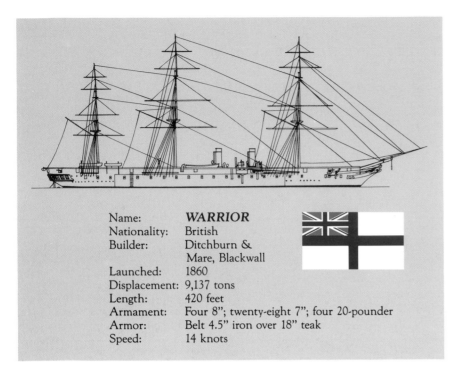

Name:	**WARRIOR**
Nationality:	British
Builder:	Ditchburn & Mare, Blackwall
Launched:	1860
Displacement:	9,137 tons
Length:	420 feet
Armament:	Four 8"; twenty-eight 7"; four 20-pounder
Armor:	Belt 4.5" iron over 18" teak
Speed:	14 knots

more than a dozen firms, and orders were placed for armored ships. *Warrior*, the first of these to be completed, joined the fleet in 1861. By an extraordinary chance this ship was never scrapped. She can be seen today, restored to something very like her original condition, in Portsmouth Dockyard.

Warrior was a much more formidable vessel than *La Gloire*. Nearly twice the size, she was iron-built, much more heavily armed, and faster. Quickly followed by a series of nine even larger ironclads, *Warrior* smartly reestablished the supremacy of the Royal Navy, consolidated by the country's greater industrial resources.

By a curious paradox the shift to iron construction and steam propulsion turned to Britain's advantage. The nation, which had established naval supremacy with timber-built square-rigged ships, was dependent on Baltic pine for masts and, after 1802, on imported oak for hulls. In 1850 Britain manufactured 2.5 million tons of iron, nearly half the world total, and the best steam coal in the world came from the seams of South Wales.

The new warships were enormously costly. Wealth generated by new industries, coupled with industrial capacity, gave advantage to the island nation in the new era of iron and steam.

Although such ships as *Warrior* were equipped with engines and a propeller, "Up Screw and Down Funnel" was standard practice once a vessel reached the open sea. The 24-foot diameter propeller had to be disconnected, and 600 men would haul on ropes to hoist it into a well beneath the poop. The funnels were telescopic.

All fighting ships used to be described as men-of-war. Only the strongest warships, those that were designed to take their place in the line sailing into battle against an enemy fleet, were ranked as line-of-battle ships. *Warrior* was intended for independent service, to catch and destroy the French ironclads, but the use of iron construction enabled her to have a hull of greater length, much longer than contemporary line-of-battle ships.

The need for two or three superimposed layers of gun decks in the old wooden ships had been overcome by the growing size and power of individual guns, and gunports had to be widely spaced in order not to diminish the strength of the protection. The new ironclads were long and low, but their guns were still disposed along the sides of the hull with limited fields of fire.

At the outbreak of the American Civil War in 1861, the Confederate forces occupied Norfolk Navy Yard. Salvaging *Merrimac*, a wooden screw frigate that had been scuttled by the Navy before departure, they set about creating a makeshift ironclad out of the surviving hull. The top deck was removed and replaced with a massive timber sloping casemate, clad on the outside with iron and projecting like a skirt well beyond the lines of the hull. This hybrid, not unlike the French floating batteries used in the Crimean War, was armed with a mixture of smooth-bore and rifled guns firing explosive shells, mounted behind ports. Her speed was a meager two or three knots.

Slow she might be, unseaworthy, and of limited endurance, but *Virginia*, as she was renamed, was very nearly unsinkable. The prospect of her steaming inexorably up the Potomac caused consternation in Washington.

The Federal authorities hastily set about finding a ship that could counter this threat. Construction was rushed through of a remarkable craft designed by John Ericsson.

Ericsson recognized the tactical advantage of mounting guns in a revolving armored turret. Not only could the same guns be used on either beam, but they could be brought to bear on almost any bearing (unless restricted by the masts and stays of sailing rig), and the guns and crews were protected from enemy fire.

The ship designed by Ericsson and built in the short space of six months mounted two massive 11" smooth-bore cannon in a single heavily armored cylindrical turret amidships. Her raft-like timber and iron hull was of shallow draft and low freeboard, and it was protected by 5" iron cladding.

She was called *Monitor*, and she gave her name to a type of shallow-draft vessel mounting turrets with heavy guns that was designed for work close to shore. Conspicuously unseaworthy, *Monitor* only narrowly succeeded in making the passage from the Hudson River to Chesapeake Bay under tow.

Virginia's first sortie from the Elizabeth River into Hampton Roads took place on March 8, 1862. She encountered a Federal frigate, whose broadside of shot simply rattled off the armored casemate. When *Virginia* fired in her turn, the explosive shells had a devastating effect on the wooden warship, setting her on fire, and causing her eventually to surrender. *Virginia* sank a second warship with her ram.

By the next day the tiny *Monitor* had arrived to confront the Confederate ironclad. The contest

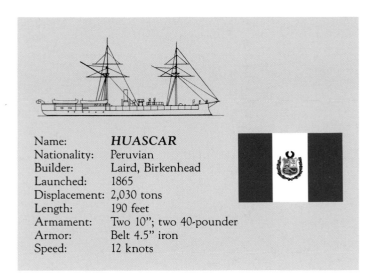

Name:	**HUASCAR**
Nationality:	Peruvian
Builder:	Laird, Birkenhead
Launched:	1865
Displacement:	2,030 tons
Length:	190 feet
Armament:	Two 10"; two 40-pounder
Armor:	Belt 4.5" iron
Speed:	12 knots

took place at point-blank range, each ship belaboring the other with shot and shell. Neither was able to penetrate the other's protection, although many men were wounded by flying splinters within the hulls. *Monitor's* captain was injured while peering through a slot in the conning tower.

It was a slow-motion fight. *Monitor's* guns took seven or eight minutes to load, and at one point she retired into shallow water to give time to bring up fresh ammunition from below. *Virginia's* broadsides came at intervals of 15 minutes. Each vessel tried ineffectually to sink the other by ramming; neither was able to inflict mortal damage on her antagonist. The outcome was inconclusive and the encounter was never renewed.

The significant feature of *Monitor* was the combination of iron cladding and the revolving turret. This led the way to future development. The Union made a specialty of the low-freeboard type of ship, and the U.S. Navy continued to hold an exaggerated regard for it right up to the end of the nineteenth century. The monitor *Miantonomoh* made a visit to European ports in 1866-67, but conditions on board in the open sea were dreadful. Waves would wash over the decks, and the hull had to be constantly battened down or risk being swamped.

Plate 10.

SHAH and *HUASCAR*

Ilo, Peru, 1877

The British iron screw frigate *Shah* can be seen going into action in a following wind. She is setting studding-sails, which are rigged on either side of the main sail, to try to increase her speed. *Shah* is firing at the renegade Peruvian ironclad *Huascar*, which has lowered her bulwarks in order to allow her turret a field of fire. The frigate is flying the signal "Cut off the enemy," which is addressed to the corvette *Amethyst* in the background.

Shots from the British ships rattled off *Huascar*'s armor plating without effect, but the mutineers were unable to get off more than five rounds from their big guns, none of which found its mark. Later in the engagement *Shah* launched a torpedo at *Huascar*, but it proved too slow to overtake the diminutive turret ship. This was the first ever use of the underwater weapon in action.

Huascar surrendered to Peruvian authorities. From 1878 to 1879 the ship saw much fighting in the wars with Chile. She was eventually captured by the Chilean Navy, and after a long and honorable service, she is preserved to this day at Talcahuano.

The Royal Navy signal code differed from International Code before 1945. Although many of the two codes' individual flags appear similar, they signify different alphabetical letters. Most tactical orders were conveyed by small groups of flags, and code books were revised every few years to accommodate changing needs.

The Confederacy, desperate to break the blockade of its ports, turned to Europe to obtain new warships. The most famous vessel acquired was the British-built *Alabama*, which had a dazzling career as a commerce raider. It is less well known that the southern states tried to create a navy of ironclads, which the North would have been powerless to stop. Fortunately for the Union, the French and British governments were able to forestall delivery of the ships.

In 1861 the Confederate agent in England placed an order with Lairds of Birkenhead for two ironclad turret ships, to be called *North Carolina* and *Mississippi*.

They were remarkable vessels. Captain Cowper Coles of the Royal Navy, another protagonist of the armored turret ship, had taken out patents for his turret design two years before. These were not the first ships to be built to his design, but they were true ocean-going vessels (although with shallow draft for operation up the Mississippi), and they were equipped with rams. The ships had a substantial forecastle and poop deck, between which there were hinged iron bulwarks amidships which could be dropped to allow the guns a clear field of fire in action. Full sailing rig was deemed necessary, but Coles devised tubular iron tripod masts in order to reduce the interference that shrouds would have caused to the turret's field of fire.

To conceal the identity of their true owners, Lairds put out that the ironclads had been ordered by Egypt, but the British government got wind of the scheme and seized them to prevent their delivery to the rebel states. They were taken into service in the Royal Navy as *Scorpion* and *Wivern*.

Coles was responsible for the design of several more ironclads built by Lairds. One of these ships, *Huascar*, can be seen to this day at the Chilean naval base of Talcahuano, south of Valparaiso. She was built in 1865 for the Republic of Peru. The country was at war with Spain, which was intent on reconquering its colonial possessions, and

Huascar was named for an Inca chief, son of the eleventh Emperor. Her design followed very closely the lines of the two Confederate ships.

Huascar sailed from England to South America in company with a broadside ironclad, *Independencia*, which had been built for Peru by Samuda on the Thames. They captured three Spanish prizes on the way, but by the time they reached the west coast the war with Spain had ended.

Twelve years later *Huascar* was seized by mutineers who were attempting to install a new caudillo named Pierola. The ship embarked on a piratical career up and down the coast, which the Peruvian government was powerless to stop. Peru appealed to Commodore de Horsey, who was in command of the Royal Navy's Pacific Station with his flagship *Shah* and the corvette *Amethyst*.

Shah was no ironclad. She was a fast iron-built steam frigate without armor protection and with her guns located in the usual way, behind ports along the sides. The origin of her design is interesting, for it was the Confederate success with raiders like *Alabama* that inspired the building of fast frigates of the *Wampanoag* class for the U.S. Navy. Concerned at the possible use of such ships as commerce raiders, the Royal Navy decided to follow suit. An interesting addition to her armament was the newly-invented Whitehead torpedo.

The encounter between *Shah* and *Huascar* was a stand-off. The British ship, after delivering a formal ultimatum in the name of the Queen, bombarded her adversary with 9" and 7" shells for two hours with practically no effect. Fortunately, the Peruvian rebels were hopelessly incompetent inside their turret and managed to get off only five rounds, none of which found its mark. A single hit with a 300-pound shell could have had fatal consequences for the frigate.

Commodore de Horsey tried a torpedo, the first time one was ever used in action. Alerted by the activity on deck, *Huascar* turned her stern to the

British ship and put on all steam. The torpedo was unable to overtake her.

Huascar's fire was concentrated on *Shah*, and the Commodore sent *Amethyst* to cut off the renegade from the shore. Nevertheless the Peruvian ironclad managed to withdraw into shallow water before the port of Ilo, where de Horsey was unable to continue bombarding her. He tried a further torpedo expedition by night, using a steam pinnace, but was unable to locate the rebel ship.

Huascar surrendered to the Peruvian authorities overnight. The British ships were scarcely damaged, but never again was the Pacific Station left without an armored ship.

In 1879 *Huascar* played an important part in the naval actions of the Nitrate War, fought between Peru and Chile over the region of Antofagasta. In a rousing engagement with the elderly wooden screw corvette *Esmeralda*, *Huascar*, after making an unsuccessful attempt to ram, was boarded by the Chilean captain. The boarding party was cut down, and a second assault was also repelled. Finally *Huascar* succeeded in sinking her adversary by ramming.

Four months later Chile took her revenge. Two Chilean ironclads, *Cochrane* and *Blanco Encalada*, encountered *Huascar*, and in the course of an hour and a half they scored more than 70 hits with 9" armor-piercing shells. The superstructure was ruined, the turret was pierced, and the captain was killed. Chilean boarders prevented the ship from being scuttled, and she was taken into Chilean service.

Huascar had a long career under the Chilean flag, taking part in the blockade of Peru and in the Chilean civil war of 1891. She remained in naval service until the 1930s, latterly as a submarine depot ship. The ironclad has been splendidly restored and is treated with the respect due to a national monument.

In a further twist to the story of the ironclad and the turret, the Chilean ironclads, which finally

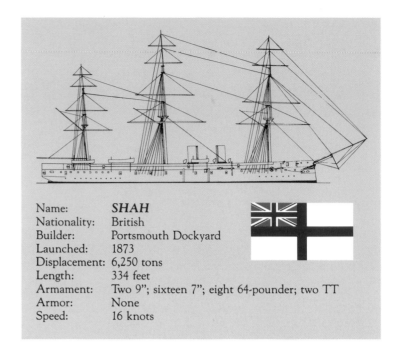

Name:	*SHAH*
Nationality:	British
Builder:	Portsmouth Dockyard
Launched:	1873
Displacement:	6,250 tons
Length:	334 feet
Armament:	Two 9"; sixteen 7"; eight 64-pounder; two TT
Armor:	None
Speed:	16 knots

overcame *Huascar*, were central-battery ships built in Britain and designed by Sir Edward Reed, Chief Constructor of the Royal Navy from 1864 to 1870. During his first years in office, he favored the central-battery layout, although the earliest ocean-going turret ships were also built for the navy during those years. Coles, the turret enthusiast, had become obsessed with his theories, and a bitter controversy was waged in press and Parliament. Finally the Admiralty gave way. Over the head of the Chief Constructor, they ordered a ship to be built along the lines so persistently advocated by Captain Coles.

This ship, *Captain*, was a much enlarged version of *Huascar*. She was designed and built by Lairds, with a full square-sail rig on tripod masts. Her two twin turrets were mounted on a deck only nine feet above water level, but like *Huascar*, she had a high forecastle and quarterdeck. She also had a central superstructure connected to the ends of the ship by bridges over the turrets.

Captain put to sea in 1870, and in September of that year she was blown over onto her beam ends and foundered in a gale in the Bay of Biscay. Most of the crew of 500 were lost, including Captain Coles. Reed, who alone had remained critical of the ship's design and stability, had resigned his post at the Admiralty two months before.

The loss of *Captain* caused serious misgivings about the whole concept of turret ships. But the inquiry showed that the fault lay with the combination of low freeboard and a full-rigged ship; the crew had been unable to shorten sail quickly enough in a sudden squall.

Interestingly, Reed himself had been responsible, before he left office, for the design of the definitive ocean-going turret ship. Construction began in 1869, before the loss of *Captain*, of a ship called *Devastation*. She dispensed entirely with sailing rig, was all iron-built, and carried her principal armament in turrets.

Devastation was the world's first true battleship. Her design finally resolved all the groping experiments to make best use of the new technologies in propulsion, construction materials, protection, and firepower.

The critical decision was the reliance on steam power alone. With the introduction of twin screws and separate engines to each shaft, it was finally possible to drop the need for sailing rig to enable a ship to be brought to port in the event of an engine breakdown. In Reed's view a high freeboard was essential so long as sea-going rig was required, but he was prepared to accept a much reduced height above waterline for a ship without masts and yards.

Devastation was a genuine sea-going ship with a displacement[1] of more than 9,000 tons. Her main deck freeboard was only 4.5 feet, but her turrets were mounted one deck higher. Effectively, the low freeboard was only at bow and stern.

Her engines gave her a speed of 14 knots, and she carried sufficient coal for a range of 4,700 miles. Her four 12" rifled guns were mounted in two twin turrets fore and aft on the center line, with wide unobstructed fields of fire over bow and stern. The compact central superstructure carried armored conning tower and bridge, two funnels, a simple pole mast, and a close-range armament of machine guns.

The engines were of horizontal double trunk design as patented by John Penn in 1845, a development of the original single trunk steam engine invented by James Watt in 1784. Steam was introduced on either side of the pistons, enabling the engine to be installed horizontally at the side of the shaft.

The whole hull was protected from bow to stern with an iron belt 10" thick and a 3" armored deck close to water level. For the first few years of her 30-year service, *Devastation* was unsinkable by any available weapon.

Evolution from this date took the form of successively bigger guns, in response to which ships were provided with ever thicker and tougher armor. The broad trend in the design of armored ships followed the pattern set by *Devastation* right on to the end of the nineteenth century.

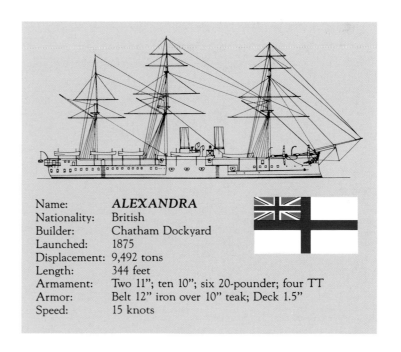

Name: **ALEXANDRA**
Nationality: British
Builder: Chatham Dockyard
Launched: 1875
Displacement: 9,492 tons
Length: 344 feet
Armament: Two 11"; ten 10"; six 20-pounder; four TT
Armor: Belt 12" iron over 10" teak; Deck 1.5"
Speed: 15 knots

Plate 11.

ALEXANDRA followed by ***AGINCOURT*** and four other ironclads through the Dardanelles, 1878

In 1877 a renewed Russian attack on the sickly Ottoman Empire, 20 years after the conclusion of the Crimean War, caused Britain to station the Mediterranean Fleet on the Turkish coast as a gesture of support. Britain feared not only Russian occupation of Constantinople and the Dardanelles, but also the presence of the Russian navy in the Eastern Mediterranean and the possible interruption of traffic to India via the Suez Canal.

When the threat became acute in February 1878, the Royal Navy was sent up the Dardanelles. Admiral Hornby, in the new battleship *Alexandra*, led five other great ironclads through the narrow passage in the teeth of a blinding snowstorm. When the fleet appeared off Constantinople, the show of force was enough to induce the Russians to climb down and negotiate a political settlement with the Turks.

Powered by vertical compound reciprocating engines, *Alexandra* could make 15 knots—for many years the fastest speed of any battleship. She was also one of the last battleships to be provided with full square-sail rig; for the run up the Dardanelles, the topmasts and upper spars were sent down, and the ship was cleared for action. The order "Keep in the Admiral's wake" is flying from the main yardarm.

Plate 12.

REDOUTABLE

Guadaloupe, 1879

Parallel with the development of the seagoing turret ship was that of the central-battery ironclad. The principal armament of the latter was concentrated amidships in an armored citadel, and designers used various means to try to improve the field of fire.

Redoutable was built during the period 1873-78. Her citadel housed four 10.8" breech-loading guns at the corners with two more in barbettes above it. She had a 10.8" bow chaser and another at the stern.

The exaggerated tumble home of the sides is typical of French design; the upper deck half the width of the hull at the waterline. The main purpose was to allow end-on fire from guns in the central battery. French warships also always seem to wear larger ensigns than those of other navies.

Redoutable was notable for the early use of steel, which was employed for much of the framing. The bow is not a ram; it was cut away to avoid damage from the forward gun.

Like many French warships, *Redoutable* was a long time under construction. She was authorized in 1872 as part of a massive building program after the defeat of 1870, but by the time she was completed in 1878, central-battery ships were becoming obsolete. Consequently, much of her career was spent on colonial stations, and she is pictured here off the island of Guadaloupe in the West Indies. Her final period of service was in Indo-China up to 1910.

CHAPTER II
GUNBOAT DIPLOMACY

In 1874 a certain Mr. Magee, British vice-consul in the port of San José, Guatemala, was seized on the orders of the military governor and subjected to a public flogging. History is silent on the nature of his offense, but the captain of an American merchant ship that happened to be in port was so outraged by the spectacle that he intervened.

Weeks later, when news of the incident finally reached the authorities in London, the Royal Navy was instructed to send ships of the Pacific Fleet to the port. The commander of the squadron sent word to the Guatemalan government that they must pay due respect to the British flag. A regiment of soldiers and a battery of artillery were obediently dispatched to San José, where salutes were fired from dawn to dusk, and an enormous sum in compensation was paid to Mr. Magee. Thereafter the British consul was held in considerable awe.

In the nineteenth century naval landing parties often played the role of policemen or emergency rescue teams, but the real reason for maintaining warships on foreign stations was to reinforce the arm of diplomacy. The term used was "protection of national interests," and it could range from evacuating nationals during an insurrection and putting out fires after an earthquake to occasional intervention by naked force.

Protection of the national flag against piracy was one of the historic reasons for creating a navy; the United States built its first frigates primarily to deal with Barbary pirates, who were attacking American ships in the Mediterranean. By the late nineteenth century, the suppression of piracy seemed like an archaic pretext for gunboat diplomacy, but this was only because the Royal Navy had effectively adopted the role of policeman on a worldwide scale. Interestingly, today piracy has revived and constitutes a very real hazard in the South China Sea off Vietnam and Malaysia, in the Sulu Sea west of the Philippines, off West Africa, and in the Caribbean. In recent times navies have been required to conduct police work in the Persian Gulf and to combat armed robbery in the South Atlantic.

The term "gunboat" was applied particularly to river craft, shallow-draft vessels designed to project a maritime nation's power inland as far as possible. The Nile, the Euphrates, the Niger, and the Irrawaddy each became the scene of riverine expeditions, but the great theater of the river gunboat was the mighty Yangtze-Kiang in China.

The first iron warships were river steamers built for the Honourable East India Company in the 1830s. The first two, *Tigris* and *Euphrates*, were ordered in 1834 to pioneer the "Overland Route" to India via Mesopotamia, and other shallow-draft vessels were constructed for service on the great rivers of India—the Indus and the Ganges.

Orders were placed in 1839 for two much larger gunboats. Named *Nemesis* and *Phlegethon*, these pretty iron paddle steamers were designed and built by Lairds of Birkenhead. Both ships made the passage to India under their own steam.

In January 1841 *Nemesis* steamed up the Yangtze, towing into action a wooden square-rigged man-of-

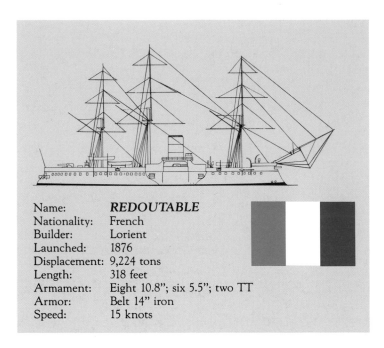

Name:	**REDOUTABLE**
Nationality:	French
Builder:	Lorient
Launched:	1876
Displacement:	9,224 tons
Length:	318 feet
Armament:	Eight 10.8"; six 5.5"; two TT
Armor:	Belt 14" iron
Speed:	15 knots

war. With an armament of two pivot-mounted 32-pounder guns and a draft of only five feet, the gunboat was more than a match for Chinese war junks and had no difficulty in penetrating up river past the antiquated shore defenses. Such was the superiority of modern weapons that for the next 100 years there was no means of preventing foreign gunboats from navigating this great river for as many as 1,400 miles through the heart of China. Special ships were built for the purpose, with their comfortable cabins shaded by civilized verandas, machine guns mounted in elevated fighting tops, and howitzers tucked away behind bulletproof shields on deck.

Coaling was the name of the game in the nineteenth-century navy, and Britain's incredible worldwide network of coal depots gave the Royal Navy its omnipotence.

James Morris in his evocative book *Pax Britannica* includes this description of a coaling station:

One such dimly comprehended possession was the island of St. Lucia, which not one Briton in a thousand could place on the map, and scarcely one in a million could pronounce properly (it should be St. Loosha). Few islands better fulfilled the dream of a tropical paradise. St. Lucia lay among the Windward Islands, looking southwards to St. Vincent and the Grenadines, washed on one side by the bluff waves of the Atlantic, on the other by the gentle Caribbean. It was a volcanic island, crowned by the striking twin peaks of the Pitons, like miniature wooded Matterhorns above the water, and most of its small expanse was covered with a delicious tropical foliage, frogs croaking, parrots brilliantly on the wing, green lagoons in shadowy recesses of jungle. The centre of the island was mountainous. Around its perimeter palm-trees leant crookedly over white beaches, and creeks ran between high brush-covered bluffs as in a hotter Devon. St. Lucia was some 3,500 miles from London. Like many an island fortress it had endured an uncertain history, and had been passed from France to Britain, Britain to France, fourteen times in all as the one Power or the other gained supremacy in the West Indies.

Castries was one of the finest natural harbours in the world, and St. Lucia was traditionally the key to the Caribbean. St. Lucia was an Imperial Naval Coaling Station and fifteen ships of the Royal Navy called at Castries in an average month. *Statio Haud Malefida Carinis* was the island's motto—the Never Unfaithful Anchorage; it was a familiar but always stirring sight to see a British warship steaming in through the narrow harbour entrance, flags flying everywhere, respectfully saluted by the passing merchantmen, and glittering with the special white and brass éclat of the North America and West Indies Station.[2]

The island of Zanzibar off the coast of East Africa was another British coaling station, and the painting of the small British cruiser *St. George* lying in the roadstead is an apt illustration of the era of Gunboat Diplomacy.

Zanzibar was the site of a Portuguese trading post founded in the early sixteenth century. Arabs from the Muscat drove out the Portuguese some 200 years later, and in 1840 it became the seat of the Sultan of Oman.

A British consul was appointed to Zanzibar in 1841. One of the principal objectives of British influence was to bring to an end the slave trade, which persisted on the east coast of Africa long after it had been suppressed on the west. Dr. John Kirk, British medical officer and later consul at Zanzibar for more than 20 years, became a close friend and adviser to Sultan Seyyid Said and his successors. An associate of Livingstone, Kirk was one of the chief architects of the suppression of slavery, and he acted jealously to preserve the independence of Zanzibar. The island became a British Protectorate in 1890. On the death of the old Sultan Hamed bin Thwain in 1896, power was seized by a faction that tried to exploit resentment against his antislavery policy.

The Royal Navy was called in, and within days four warships assembled off the waterfront: *St. George*, the flagship, and two smaller cruisers named *Philomel* and *Raccoon*, together with the gunboat *Thrush*. (Ship's names of the Victorian Navy have an inescapable charm. Other Royal Navy ships included *Tickler*, *Cheerful*, *Cuckoo*, *Dapper*, *Harebell*, *Harpy*, *Fidget*, and *Flirt*.)

The British Resident delivered the usual ultimatum; when it expired the ships cleared for action. Guns were trained on the town, and in due course fire was directed on the rebels who had taken over the Sultan's armed yacht and the Palace. This brought the revolt to an end within 30 minutes, and the new Sultan was duly installed.

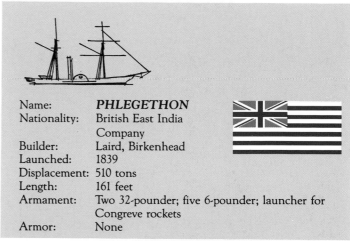

Name:	**PHLEGETHON**
Nationality:	British East India Company
Builder:	Laird, Birkenhead
Launched:	1839
Displacement:	510 tons
Length:	161 feet
Armament:	Two 32-pounder; five 6-pounder; launcher for Congreve rockets
Armor:	None

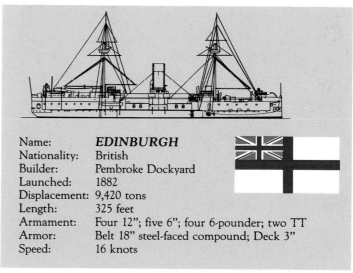

Name:	**EDINBURGH**
Nationality:	British
Builder:	Pembroke Dockyard
Launched:	1882
Displacement:	9,420 tons
Length:	325 feet
Armament:	Four 12"; five 6"; four 6-pounder; two TT
Armor:	Belt 18" steel-faced compound; Deck 3"
Speed:	16 knots

The tall cool house built by Sultan Barghash for Sir John Kirk still stands on a headland to the south of the town, surrounded by the arboretum that Kirk cultivated. It was from there that the expeditions of Burton, Speke, Stanley, and Lugard set out to explore the interior of East Africa.

St. George was based at Simonstown, an enchantingly English town on the east side of the Cape Peninsula near Cape Town. In 1895 she took part in the Third Ashanti War, carrying a naval brigade to the Gold Coast, and in 1897 she landed a naval expedition at Benin to suppress a native ruler who had been committing atrocities on the borders of Nigeria.

Plate 13.

EDINBURGH
South Queensferry, Firth of Forth, 1888

The battleship *Edinburgh* was guardship at Queensferry during the time of construction of the Forth Bridge. This astonishing cantilever structure celebrated its centenary in March 1990, and it still carries the main railway line from London to the north of Scotland.

Edinburgh is flying the guardship pendant and a signal ordering another ship to weigh anchor. Someone seems to be having a little difficulty with one of the ships' boats at the starboard boat boom. The battleship is painted in the smart Victorian livery of black, white, and buff, with red boot topping edged in white. In 1902 the ship's coloring was converted to the familiar battleship grey.

Edinburgh is an interesting example of the period of transition in design from the square-rigged ironclad, such as *Alexandra*, to the pre-Dreadnought battleship. It was a period of many experiments and some bizarre designs, efforts to combine the invulnerability of the low-freeboard monitor and the advantages of mounting the guns in turrets with the sea-keeping qualities of more traditional hull layouts. The problem was further confused by lingering doubts about the wisdom of abandoning sail altogether and becoming hostage to the reliability of engines and the availability of coal supplies.

Plate 14.

ST. GEORGE

Zanzibar, 1896

The Sultan of Zanzibar is being rowed ashore after paying a ceremonial visit to the flagship of Rear-Admiral Sir Harry Rawson, Commander-in-Chief of the Cape and West Africa Station.

A gift of Queen Victoria, the Zanzibar State Barge, with its scarlet-coated oarsmen, resembles the state barges used by British sovereigns on the Thames (and which can be seen in the National Maritime Museum at Greenwich).

To the left the ruined Sultan's Palace, with its tall flagstaff flying a blood-red flag, can be seen. Behind the barge is the Bet-el-Ajaib, whose centerpiece is a tower built as a lighthouse and whose clock still keeps time according to the Arab day, which begins at dawn.

Behind the cruiser lies the fort, and on the extreme right can be seen the offices of the Eastern & South African Telegraph Company, a typical nineteenth-century colonial building with cast-iron verandas. The ship's signal hoist reads, "I am carrying mails. I have no doctor on board."

Zanzibar and the adjoining island of Pemba remain to this day the chief world source of supply for cloves, and the ancient trade by dhow to the Persian Gulf continues to follow the seasonal monsoon. Some of these lateen-rigged vessels can be seen on the left of the picture.

A celebrated event in the worldwide struggle for naval shore facilities was the typhoon at Apia. In 1889 Germany and the United States stood eyeball-to-eyeball in the Samoan Islands of the southwest Pacific. Each country had sent several warships "to protect their national interests." The British cruiser *Calliope* was sent to keep a watching brief.

On March 16 one of the worst typhoons of the century hit the islands, and six of the warships—three German and three American—were washed ashore with the loss of 150 lives. *Calliope* alone managed to steam out of harbor in the face of mountainous waves and ride out the storm in safety.

The diplomatic confrontation resulted in the division of the island group; the eastern half fell under American administration, and the western, including the port of Apia, under German. Each power established a coaling station on their sector.

Perhaps the most unlikely coaling station was that established by the British in 1846 on the tiny island of Labuan, which lies immediately offshore Brunei Bay on the northwest coast of the great East Indies island of Borneo. Seams of coal, discovered on Labuan, were worked in the vain hope that they would prove a commercially exploitable source of supply for merchant shipping, while at the same time providing for ships of the Royal Navy's China Squadron. The idea was the brainchild of the legendary James Brooke, who later became the first of the White Rajahs of nearby Sarawak. He visualized a prosperous entrepôt along the lines of Singapore and Hong Kong.

Unfortunately the island turned out to be a pestilential swamp, so unhealthy that miners struggled hopelessly in the torrid climate, and successive generations of Colonial Servants died like flies. The miniature port of Victoria never came to resemble the prosperous port of the same name on Hong Kong island.

A hundred years later during the Second World War, the whole of Borneo was occupied by the Japanese. When news was received of the American assault on Leyte Island in the Philippines in October 1944, the main Japanese fleet was sent from Singapore to Labuan. Seven battleships, thirteen cruisers, and escorting destroyers arrived in Brunei Bay, and from there the Japanese sailed on October 22 for the Battle of Leyte Gulf. *Musashi* and *Yamato*, the two greatest armored ships ever built, were among their number.

The age of Gunboat Diplomacy affords countless examples of intervention. There was no pressure more explicit than the arrival of a warship.

One of the most notorious was the Agadir Crisis of 1911. It is difficult to reconstruct the tensions that were aroused by the stationing of the German gunboat *Panther* off the Moroccan town of Agadir. She displaced only 1,000 tons and carried two 4.1" guns.

Continuing French expansion in North Africa precipitated a competing claim by Germany to some kind of presence in the region. Germany had already established colonial administrations in a number of Pacific island territories, as well as in East, Southwest and West Africa, and she possessed a Treaty Port in China. Maybe Germany's purpose for sending *Panther* was to try to overawe France or to test the strength of the newly formed Entente.

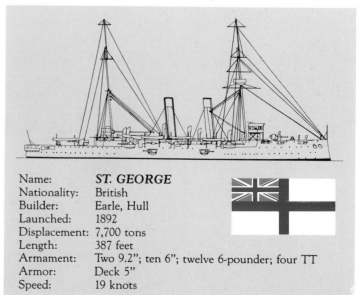

Name:	**ST. GEORGE**
Nationality:	British
Builder:	Earle, Hull
Launched:	1892
Displacement:	7,700 tons
Length:	387 feet
Armament:	Two 9.2"; ten 6"; twelve 6-pounder; four TT
Armor:	Deck 5"
Speed:	19 knots

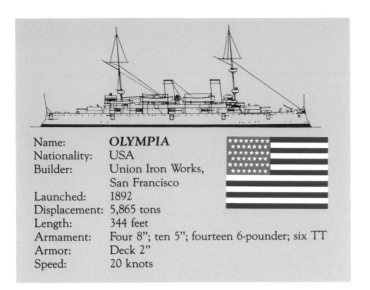

Name:	**OLYMPIA**
Nationality:	USA
Builder:	Union Iron Works, San Francisco
Launched:	1892
Displacement:	5,865 tons
Length:	344 feet
Armament:	Four 8"; ten 5"; fourteen 6-pounder; six TT
Armor:	Deck 2"
Speed:	20 knots

Something of the kind was tried by Hitler in central Europe in the 1930s: a provocation to test the resolve of the opposition.

In the event the British government finally took courage to speak out firmly. Britain would not fail to come to the aid of its ally France. Supported by mobilization of the Royal Navy, the warning was sufficient to cause Germany to back down. Once the crisis had passed, Britain sent an emissary to Germany in an attempt to cool the growing antagonism and to scale down the naval arms race. He was not successful.

As coal gave way to oil as the fuel for warships, the interest of naval powers switched to sources of supply. In 1914 25 percent of the world's oil supply came from Mexico, and it was the principal source of oil fuel used by the Royal Navy.

General Huerta, who had seized power in Mexico, was seen by President Woodrow Wilson in much the same light as Noriega and Ortega have been perceived by recent U.S. Presidents. Wilson warned Huerta not to stand for election (on the grounds that the poll would surely be rigged), and the "Contras" led by General Carranza were provided with arms and logistic support.

Germany, sensing an opportunity to throttle the supply of oil to Britain, struck a bargain with Huerta and shipped machine guns and rifles to Mexico. On April 6, 1914, the U.S. Navy dispatch vessel *Dolphin*, anchored off the Mexican port of Tampico, put some sailors ashore who were promptly arrested. While Mexican authorities released them very shortly, Admiral Mayo demanded an apology and a 21-gun salute, both of which were backed up by an ultimatum issued by Washington. Days passed without action, but the arrival at Veracruz of the first of the German munitions ships triggered the whole situation.

Wilson gave orders to stop German guns from being delivered to Huerta. The auxiliary cruiser *Prairie* turned back the German merchant ship and landed marines who took possession of the Customs House and other key installations at Veracruz. Mexican troops and civilians opened fire on the invaders from the fort and the windows of their houses, and in the ensuing bombardment of the town by the U.S. Navy, 145 lives were lost.

The Germans quietly landed their supplies at ports further south, but the munitions were not enough to save Huerta. Overwhelmed by his antagonist Carranza, the dictator fled. The ship that took him to exile was the German cruiser *Dresden*, thoughtfully supplied by the Kaiser.

The end of the gunboat era can be pinpointed to 1949, when a communist army caught a British frigate hundreds of miles up the Yangtze. *Amethyst* was taking supplies to the British Embassy in Chungking, which was then the capital of China. The Red Army evidently supposed that the warship was there to assist Chiang Kai-Shek's forces in preventing the crossing of the river barrier. Heavy artillery was brought up to the bank, and the unarmored frigate was held at bay for weeks until she managed to make a midnight escape.

After this incident the presence of a single warship ceased to cut much ice. When Iran's Premier Mossadeq seized the giant Anglo-Iranian oil refinery at Abādān in 1951, the arrival of a British cruiser in the Tigris had little influence on events.

Plate 15.

OLYMPIA

Hong Kong, 1898

Immediately before the outbreak of the Spanish-American War in 1898, Commodore Dewey's flagship, the protected cruiser *Olympia*, was visiting Hong Kong. She is seen at dusk with the handsome Victorian dockyard buildings in the background.

At the beginning of the war, Commodore Dewey sailed for the Spanish colony of the Philippines. He commanded the East Asiatic Squadron, which comprised a mixed force of four cruisers, two gunboats, and a revenue cutter. Admiral Montojo's squadron of seven

obsolete Spanish warships, which lay at anchor under the guns of Cavite, was sunk without casualty to the American ships. Dewey then blockaded Manila for four months until the U.S. Army arrived to take possession.

In her subsequent career the cruiser served as flagship of the North Atlantic Squadron, flagship of the Patrol Force after America entered the First World War, and flagship of the Mediterranean Squadron in 1918.

Olympia, still afloat, is one of only three pre-First World War cruisers in the world.

She lies at Penn's Landing on the Delaware River in downtown Philadelphia, where she is maintained as a historic monument. The two other old cruisers are the Greek *Averoff*, located at Póros Island, and the Russian *Aurora* on the River Neva in Leningrad.

Plate 16.

TAKASAGO

Dartmouth, 1898

The tidal reaches of the River Dart, on the south coast of Devon, wind toward the sea between steep slopes heavily clad in beech woods. The town of Dartmouth is completely sheltered; clinging to the hillside, it faces across a secluded deepwater anchorage toward the houses of Kingswear.

The port has always been a safe haven, although a difficult one to enter. For 20 years the lavender-hulled ships of Donald Currie's Castle Line put in here to collect passengers and mail before setting out for the Cape of Good Hope.

In May 1898 the Japanese Navy's protected cruiser *Takasago*, newly delivered from the Armstrong yard at Elswick, called at Dartmouth and lay at moorings in the Bight. No doubt she was picking up Japanese cadets, who had completed their training in *Britannia*. The Royal Navy College was then housed in two old wooden three-deckers, *Britannia* and *Hindostan*, which can be seen moored off Sandquay in the background.

Takasago was one of a large body of Elswick cruisers built for foreign navies during that period, and she is a good example of the genre. Her sister ship *Chacabuco* served in the Chilean navy until 1952.

CHAPTER III

ARMSTRONG OF ELSWICK

The world's airlines look first to Seattle for their big jets. In the same way the navies of the world used to turn to Armstrong of Elswick for their armored ships.

Sir William Armstrong is representative of the era. Born in 1810, he trained as a solicitor but pursued an interest in innovative engineering. He had the caution of the true scientist coupled with the vision to appreciate the practical application of new ideas. Armstrong was a friend of Joseph Swan, the pioneer of electric lighting, and his house was possibly the first in the world to be lit by electric light. It was also equipped with its own hydroelectric plant, hydraulic lifts, and internal telephone system. In middle life Armstrong gave up his legal practice in order to start an engineering works for the manufacture of hydraulic lifts and cranes.

In 1854 Britain and France went to war with Russia and landed troops in the Crimea. The troops were armed with Minié and Enfield muzzle-loading rifles, but the artillery consisted of smooth-bore cannon little different from those used in the Napoleonic wars. Armstrong decided it was time for something better. Accidents were common with early breech-loading guns, and after their first introduction to warships in 1858, they were replaced in the Royal Navy by muzzle-loading rifled guns that fired shells which had studs in the base to mesh with the rifling. The Armstrong works at Elswick, four miles upriver from the center of Newscastle-on-Tyne, became one of the foremost gun factories in the world.

Year by year Armstrong consolidated its reputation, first for armaments and then for armor plate and armored ships.

In 1873 the Italian navy placed an order with Armstrong for four 12.5" (38-ton) guns for each of two new battleships: *Duilio* and *Dandolo*. The company persuaded the Italians to supersede the order successively with 15" (50-ton) and finally with monstrous 17.7" (100-ton) guns. Armored to resist gunfire from similar weapons, *Duilio* and *Dandolo* became the first warships in the world to be armored with steel, 22"-thick plates made by the French company Creusot.

No matter that recharging the muzzle-loaders between shots might take 15 minutes; in theory, ships like this could sink anything afloat, and no gun in the Royal Navy could penetrate their armor. Britain was provoked into building a comparable warship. In 1874 the battleship *Inflexible* was laid down at Portsmouth. Armed with 16"-caliber Armstrong guns, *Inflexible* was protected by no less than a 24" thickness of armor plate, the heaviest ever carried in a ship.

The introduction of slow-burning powder led to the evolution of guns with longer barrels; a long-drawn explosion could achieve higher muzzle velocity and thus greater range, accuracy, and penetration. *Inflexible*'s guns were too long to be loaded from within the turret, so they had to be depressed below a glacis built into the deck. By 1879 techniques of gun manufacture and breech design had developed sufficiently to enable breech-loaders to be reintroduced in the Royal Navy; Armstrong mechanism and Armstrong guns were adopted.

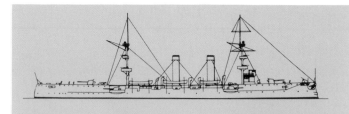

Name:	*TAKASAGO*
Nationality:	Japanese
Builder:	Armstrong, Elswick
Launched:	1897
Displacement:	4,160 tons
Length:	387 feet
Armament:	Two 8"; ten 4.7"; twelve 12-pounder; five TT
Armor:	Deck 2"
Speed:	23 knots

Elevated to the peerage, Lord Armstrong employed Norman Shaw to design a marvelous country house. The house is named Cragside and it stands like a faery castle set amongst rhododendrons on a hillside at the edge of the Northumberland moors. Clients were entertained in Tennysonian surroundings; weekend parties included Ministers of Marine, Admirals, the Shah of Persia, the King of Siam, and the Prince of Wales.

For 40 years the slips at Elswick supplied armored ships for the world. One after another they were taken down to the sea through the heart of the smoking city of Newcastle. Crowds turned out to watch and to cheer as the great black ships were eased gently between the piers of the High Level Bridge; topmasts could not be stepped until they were safely through. Standing at the scene today it seems an unlikely feat.

By 1880 the threat of attack on armored ships by fast, small craft armed with torpedoes was a growing cause for concern. The introduction of integral cartridge and shell enabled Armstrong guns of 3" to 6" caliber to achieve greatly increased rates of fire. At the limited range then envisaged for fleet actions, the smaller guns were also expected to do great destruction to the unarmored ends of larger ships.

Armstrong advocated the building of cruisers that would be much faster than current types, armed with quick-firers but dispensing with the heavy armored belt. They were to rely on speed for survival, plus a full-length armored protective deck and thorough underwater subdivision.

Unable to convince the Admiralty, he built a 3,000-ton cruiser along these lines anyway in 1884. She was sold to Peru and named *Esmeralda.*

In the course of the next 20 years, the Elswick cruiser became something of a speciality. Slender, efficient and long-lived, eight cruisers were supplied to Japan, five to Chile, and others to Argentina, Italy, Turkey, and Brazil, as well as to the British Admiralty. Two under construction for Brazil were purchased by the United States at the time of the Spanish-American War. Some of them were even built on speculation and sold on the stocks or when complete.

To prolong their endurance between docking, many of these ships were built with teak sheathing over the steel hull and coppered. In the absence of anti-fouling paints, unsheathed steel bottoms would rapidly foul with barnacles and marine growth, particularly in the tropics, so Royal Navy ships for use on the China Station were always sheathed in this way. The First Lord of the Admiralty remarked that without proper sheathing "an iron vessel on a tropical station would soon have a bottom like a lawyer's wig."

William White was "warship designer and manager" of Armstrong from 1882 to 1885, when he was appointed Director of Naval Construction at the Admiralty. In the latter post he was mainly responsible for the evolution of the pre-Dreadnought battleship as a universal type. At Elswick he was followed by Philip Watts, who again stepped into White's shoes at the Admiralty in 1902. These two men, the most eminent naval architects in the era of the armored ship, were both knighted for public service.

Elswick built all kinds of warships. Many were

destined for the Royal Navy, culminating in the 28,000-ton battleship *Malaya* completed in 1915. But it was for foreign navies that the yard became most celebrated. Japan was Armstrong's best customer, and the most illustrious ship built at Elswick was *Mikasa*, Admiral Togo's flagship at the Battle of Tsushima. In 1902, two years after Lord Armstrong's death, the Japanese battleship made her journey through Newcastle to the sea. *Mikasa* survives to this day as the only pre-Dreadnought battleship in the world, preserved as a national monument at Yokosuka. She occupies a place of honor equivalent to that of *Victory* at Portsmouth or *Constitution* at Charlestown Navy Yard in Boston.

Also in 1902, growing rivalry in South America gave rise to an order by Chile for two battleships to counter the acquisition by Argentina of Italian armored cruisers. A slump in nitrate prices led to Chile's cancellation, and when it became known that Russia was in the market for the battleships, the British government intervened and bought them. Originally to be named *Constitucion* and *Libertad*, they entered the Royal Navy as *Swiftsure* and *Triumph*, but both were known throughout the lower deck as "Ocupado" and "Vacante," the Spanish words that remained inscribed on the hardware of the ships' lavatory doors. *Swiftsure* and *Triumph* were rated as Second Class battleships and served mainly on the China Station.

Four years later, Brazil ordered a pair of battleships in Britain, one of which was to be built at Elswick. In the euphoria generated by booming prices for coffee and rubber, Brazil aspired to become the premier naval power in Latin America. *Minas Geraes* and *São Paulo* were formidable ships, the world's strongest Dreadnoughts when they were first completed in 1910. Many found it difficult to understand what Brazil should want with such warships, and there was widespread speculation that she was acting as front for another power.

Not to be overawed, Argentina shopped for a bargain. She finally placed orders in the United States for two Dreadnoughts, distinctly larger and better protected than those built for Brazil, at the very moment when the Brazilian battleships were crossing the Atlantic on delivery. The South American Dreadnought Race was under way.

Armored ships had long been symbols of status, and competition in ordering or buying cast-off ships was not a new phenomenon. Significantly, the ships were often the target of take-over bids by revolutionary groups; control of a major naval unit could well lead to mastery of the state.

Brazil was determined not to be outdone by Argentina. Foreign attachés were astonished when she placed an order with Armstrong in 1910 for yet a third Dreadnought, the *Rio de Janeiro*. This ship was to carry no fewer than seven turrets with fourteen 12" guns, the greatest number ever mounted on a ship. Years later when she took her place as the last ship in the British battle line at Jutland, observers reported that the sheet of flame from her broadside was awe inspiring.

Armstrong secured the Brazilian order by sending out its naval architect, Sir Eustace Tennyson D'Eyncourt. He took passage to Rio with a variety of drawings, thrashed out alternative designs, drew fresh plans overnight, and presented them triumphantly the following day.

45

Plate 17.

RESOLUTION

Cowes Roads,
Isle of Wight, 1898

Resolution lies off the Royal Yacht Squadron clubhouse at Cowes Castle. Designed by Sir William White, the most masterly of Victorian naval architects, she was one of eight *Royal Sovereign*-class battleships and was completed in 1893. Her principal armament was mounted in open barbettes. The reduction in weight compared with turrets enabled the guns to be placed higher above water level, and the class had much greater freeboard than turret ships such as *Colossus*, which can be seen in the distance. As a consequence the *Royal Sovereign*s were far more seaworthy, they could maintain speed in a seaway, and they provided a superior platform for the guns.

A 56-foot pinnace, which was capable of carrying 14" torpedoes, is being hoisted off the boat deck, and a delicate gig is slung on *Resolution*'s starboard quarter. A smart black steam yacht lies at the after brow, where she has just landed a party of important visitors who are being greeted on the battleship's quarterdeck. On the left is a spritsail barge (Thames barge); in the foreground, a steam picketboat.

Within 12 months Brazilian ardor for the ship had cooled. A mutiny had occurred in *Minas Geraes*, coffee prices had slumped, and there had been a change of government, so *Rio de Janeiro* was put on the market. The Turkish government stepped in. Funds were raised by public subscription, and the monster battleship was bought and renamed *Sultan Osman I*. As she approached completion, however, there was growing threat of general European war, and British authorities delayed her delivery to Turkey on various pretexts. When British involvement in the war seemed inescapable, the ship was seized, together with another Dreadnought being built for the Turkish navy by Vickers at Barrow.

While Brazil had given up acquiring its third Dreadnought, the spirit of South American rivalry was not yet exhausted. Chile regarded the American-built Argentine ships with concern, and in 1911 the Chilean government placed orders with Armstrong for two battleships with ten 14" guns, sufficient to outweigh any ship then on the stocks.

These two ships, *Almirante Latorre* and *Almirante Cochrane*, were under construction at Elswick when war broke out in Europe. The former ship was purchased by Britain, completed, and renamed *Canada*. A splendid ship, she was technically the equal of any in the Royal Navy. After the war she was refurbished and delivered to Chile, where she remained the principal unit of the fleet until her retirement in 1958.

Immediately after the attack on Pearl Harbor, when eight battleships were put out of service, the United States made an offer to purchase *Almirante Latorre* from Chile. The American request was refused, so the ex-*Canada* never had an opportunity to serve as a unit in the U.S. Navy.

Almirante Cochrane was not laid down until 1913, because the shipyard had to wait for the slip vacated by *Rio de Janeiro*. Work was suspended in 1914 due to the war. She was eventually completed in 1920 as the aircraft carrier *Eagle*. Chile negotiated for her

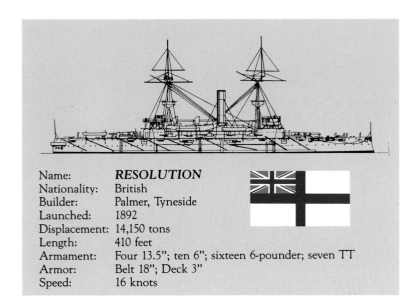

Name:	**RESOLUTION**
Nationality:	British
Builder:	Palmer, Tyneside
Launched:	1892
Displacement:	14,150 tons
Length:	410 feet
Armament:	Four 13.5"; ten 6"; sixteen 6-pounder; seven TT
Armor:	Belt 18"; Deck 3"
Speed:	16 knots

reinstatement as a battleship, but the request proved impracticable. The idea of substituting two *Invincible*-class battle cruisers was mooted, and in the end the Chilean navy settled for the one battleship.

In the meantime, Brazil had once again approached Armstrong, and in 1913 designs were prepared for another Dreadnought to take the place of *Rio de Janeiro*, one that would be superior to *Almirante Latorre*. Intentions for *Riachuelo* ranged from twelve 14" to ten 16" guns, but the outbreak of war intervened, and the project remained no more than a fantasy.

Shipbuilding continues on Tyneside. The shipyard of Swan Hunter, Wigham Richardson downriver at Wallsend built the famous Cunarder *Mauretania* in 1906. The firm is constructs warships, including the last two aircraft carriers to be built for the Royal Navy. Armstrong, however, merged with its rival Vickers. Since Vickers' new yard at Barrow-in-Furness had better access to the sea than the Elswick facility, major construction was transferred to the former location. In recent years nuclear-powered submarines have entered the water in the Irish Sea. Nothing shows today at Elswick to tell of its place of pride in the era of the armored ship.

Plate 18.

ASKOLD

Bahrain, 1902

The protected cruiser *Askold*, built in Germany for the Russian Navy, was delivered in 1901. En route to join the Pacific Squadron at Vladivostok, she passed through the Suez Canal and called at various Gulf ports on the way. She is portrayed at Bahrain, raising steam preparatory to departure.

Askold was the only warship in the world with five funnels. Her appearance caused a sensation in the Emirates, where the potency of a ship was measured by the number of its funnels. A British four-funneled cruiser on a subsequent visit to the same ports was inspired to rig two false canvas ones, complete with working steam pipes.

Askold fought the Japanese at the Battle of the Yellow Sea in August 1904. When hits on the flagship threw the main body of the Russian fleet into disarray, the Cruiser Division carried on with the intended breakout. *Askold*'s funnels were damaged, resulting in greatly increased coal consumption, so she was unable to make Vladivostok and was obliged to put in to Shanghai, where she was interned.

Released at the end of the Russo-Japanese War, *Askold* fought against Germany in the First World War in the Pacific, the Mediterranean, and the Arctic.

During the Bolshevik Revolution she was seized by the British at Murmansk, and her guns were mounted on an armored train used by Admiral Kolchak's White Russian Forces. The cruiser was returned to the Soviet government in 1921.

CHAPTER IV

CAPTAIN MAHAN AND
THE ISTHMIAN CANAL

In 1890 the President of the U.S. Naval War College, Captain Alfred Thayer Mahan, published a book called *The Influence of Sea Power on History 1660-1783*. It caused a sensation. Theodore Roosevelt became an enthusiastic disciple of his ideas, Harvard and Yale conferred honorary degrees, Mahan was invited to publish articles in the influential monthly magazines, he was honored and fêted in Germany and in England, and his work was studied in Japan.

Mahan believed that sea power conferred the ability to apply military force globally, and that this had been the decisive factor in achieving worldwide control and national prosperity, demonstrably British. Mahan articulated a theory out of a state of affairs that was already apparent, hence the instant acclaim. He advocated, of course, the creation of an ocean-going navy for the United States and, as a necessary support for this new navy, the annexation of coaling bases in Hawaii and Cuba and the creation of an Isthmian canal.

By the time of Mahan's book, the railroad had been driven from coast to coast in the United States, and the time had come to raise the American vision beyond the ocean horizons. A strong tradition countered this belief. Many people held that the new republic had no part in the power game, that the United States had been founded with the intention of turning its back on the rivalries that governed events in Europe. There were those who held that America stood for more noble and more enlightened values.

But the time for expanding U.S. interests was ripe. The Spanish empire in America and the Pacific was disintegrating. The burgeoning industrial and financial resources of America provided new-found means. Theodore Roosevelt—vigorous, self-confident, and chauvinistic—had written a book on American naval history, and he was captivated by Mahan's thesis.

America started building. Her first two battleships, *Maine* and *Texas*, were authorized in 1886 but not comissioned until 1895. *Maine*, designed as an armored cruiser, was rerated as a battleship before completion, and plans were abandoned to have her rigged for sail.

Early in 1898 *Maine* was sent to Cuba "to safeguard American interests." Spanish authorities were facing an insurgency aimed at securing home rule for the island, and there was growing sentiment in the United States in favor of the revolutionary movement. There were even those who saw this last remaining fragment of the Spanish-American empire as a natural candidate for further addition to the United States.

While lying in the harbor at Havana, *Maine* suffered a massive explosion, which sank the ship and killed 260 of the crew. The whole forward part of the vessel was destroyed.

The U.S. Navy attributed the cause to the detonation of a mine placed under the ship's hull. Whipped up by the Hearst Press, public opinion was inflamed, and Congress was urged toward war with Spain. The hue and cry drowned the voices of any who might have doubted that the Spanish

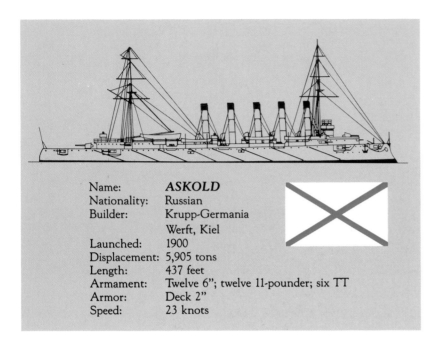

Name:	**ASKOLD**
Nationality:	Russian
Builder:	Krupp-Germania Werft, Kiel
Launched:	1900
Displacement:	5,905 tons
Length:	437 feet
Armament:	Twelve 6"; twelve 11-pounder; six TT
Armor:	Deck 2"
Speed:	23 knots

Ordered to break the blockade, the Spanish Admiral steamed bravely out to meet the enemy. A torrent of fire met his ships as they emerged. The Americans expended 8,000 rounds and achieved only 120 hits, but they were enough. The older Spanish ships were set on fire. The new Spanish cruiser, *Cristobal Colon*, survived the bombardment but ran ashore for lack of coal.

In the Far East Commodore Dewey had been replenishing at Hong Kong. At the outbreak of the Spanish-American War, he steamed to the Philippines, where he found two elderly Spanish cruisers and five gunboats. Sweeping into Manila Bay with a far more powerful squadron, he effortlessly sank the enemy ships as they lay under the guns of Cavite. Dewey's worst moment came with the subsequent arrival on the scene of the armored cruiser *Kaiser*, commanded by the German Admiral von Diederichs, whose orders were to assert German claims to the former Spanish-Pacific possessions.

As a result of the war, Spain gave up sovereignty over Cuba, and Guantánamo became an American base. The United States acquired the Philippines, Guam, and Puerto Rico, and at the same time the United States annexed the Hawaiian Islands. The Germans had to make do with the Carolinas, the Marianas, and the Marshall Islands.

Ferdinand de Lesseps, builder of the Suez Canal, which was completed in 1869, headed an ambitious undertaking launched in 1880 to cut a sea-level canal through Panama. The task was incomparably more difficult than at Suez. One reason was topography; the canal had to cut through the Continental Divide 500 feet above sea level and negotiate a torrid, jungle-covered landscape intersected by a river that was subjected to drastic floods.

While the engineering problems were unprecedented, the French company confronted even more serious difficulties. Chief among these were tropical diseases, principally malaria and yellow fever, whose

authorities were likely to have been responsible.

In 1912, long after the conclusion of the Spanish-American War, the wreck of the battleship *Maine* was raised and carefully surveyed. In recent years a technical evaluation of the evidence concluded that the source of the explosion was internal, most likely a fire in a coal bunker, which caused the explosion of an adjoining magazine. Such fires had been reported earlier.

The Spanish cruiser squadron that was in the Atlantic in 1898 took refuge in the harbor of Santiago de Cuba. The U.S. Army and Marines invaded the island, and operations on land went slowly, but in spite of ill-feeling between admirals, the naval war was a resounding success.

Spanish opposition was not formidable. The squadron holed up in Santiago comprised three obsolete cruisers, two destroyers, and an incomplete new ship, which lacked her principal armament.

origins and treatment were not as yet understood. The climate was appalling, and disease cut down the unacclimatized work force year after year.

Repeatedly, estimates of time and cost proved to have been inadequate, and by 1889 the attempt to raise yet more funds exhausted the patience and the resources of French business. The construction of the canal was by far the world's largest financial enterprise up to that time. The French company was eventually forced out of business by chicanery, but the fundamental cause of its failure in Panama was an insufficient appreciation of the magnitude of the task. More than 20,000 men died in the attempt.

Determined that a canal should be built and that it should be an American one, Theodore Roosevelt strode into the breach. A ship making passage from New York to San Francisco via Cape Horn traveled 13,000 miles; via Panama, the distance decreased to only 5,300. In the absence of a canal, the United States would have needed a fleet in each ocean sufficient to face an enemy for more than a month before hope of reinforcement by ships from the other coast.

The United States bought the concession granted to the French canal company, together with the half-completed works. The Colombian government tried to hold out for better terms, but, after some

Plate 19.

ILLUSTRIOUS

Corfu, 1902

The battleship *Illustrious* lies off the Palaión Frouríon at Corfu in 1902. The Greek national flag flies over the citadel, which was built to defend the seaward approach to the town during the days when Corfu was a Venetian possession.

The battleship is flying the "gin pendant," R.P.C., which means "Request the Pleasure of your Company" at 1800 hours. Gin and angostura bitters were *de rigueur*.

Features of interest are the lack of flare at the bow, the tumble home to the hull amidships, billboards cut into the upper deck for accommodating anchors, the boat booms rigged on both sides, anti-torpedo-net booms folded against the hull, the twin ocher-colored funnels, delicate bridge structure with semaphore signaling arms on the wings, the tall white-painted chart house, and the guns mounted in fighting tops on the masts.

From 1816 to 1864 Corfu was a British Protectorate, part of the Hebdomanian Federation of seven Ionian islands. The first Lord High Commissioner built the Palace of St. Michael and St. George, a stately official residence of Maltese sandstone on the Spianada, or esplanade. The Spianada is public garden, promenade, parade ground, and cricket field.

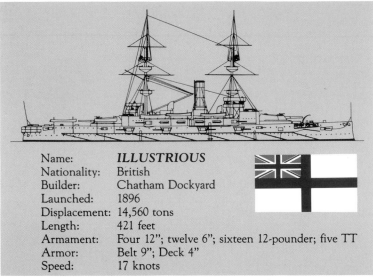

Name: **ILLUSTRIOUS**
Nationality: British
Builder: Chatham Dockyard
Launched: 1896
Displacement: 14,560 tons
Length: 421 feet
Armament: Four 12"; twelve 6"; sixteen 12-pounder; five TT
Armor: Belt 9"; Deck 4"
Speed: 17 knots

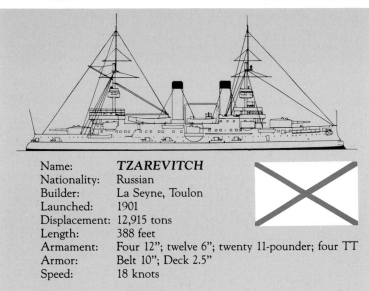

Name: **TZAREVITCH**
Nationality: Russian
Builder: La Seyne, Toulon
Launched: 1901
Displacement: 12,915 tons
Length: 388 feet
Armament: Four 12"; twelve 6"; twenty 11-pounder; four TT
Armor: Belt 10"; Deck 2.5"
Speed: 18 knots

fast footwork, the province of Panama seceded. The new country was instantly recognized by the United States, and the U.S. gunboat *Nashville* intervened to prevent the secessionists from being crushed. Panama granted the United States complete control over the Canal Zone, and in 1904 construction was resumed.

Vital to the success of the American enterprise was the identification of the malarial and yellow-fever mosquitoes and the widespread measures undertaken to control them.

The engineering works were tackled with masterly invention. An enormous freshwater reservoir, the world's largest artificial lake, was created in the center of the isthmus, where it was kept brimming by the region's torrential rain. Thus the whole problem of floods was harnessed to useful effect. Access to the lake was gained by ascending a series of locks, constantly replenished by fresh water, which raised ships on their passage from one ocean to the other. Cutting through the watershed at Culebra proved to be a labor of Sisyphus; treacherous subsoil caused heartbreaking landslides during construction and for years after the completion of the canal. The hills on either side of the canal were cut back at ever shallower angles until the volume of material removed was nearly three times what had been initially calculated. Dredging and measures for stabilization are still required to this day.

On August 3, 1914, the first ship passed through the canal, but the world's attention was focused on events in Europe. A major landslide in 1915 closed the canal, and it was not opened for general traffic until 1920.

The Panama Canal locks were built on such a generous scale that they have never needed to be enlarged or renewed. Before the advent of the nuclear-powered aircraft carrier, all American warships were designed to pass through them, and the existence of the canal has been an essential element in naval dispositions since 1914.

Panama is still regarded as a critical link in defense strategy, no less important to Washington than Suez was to London's eyes. The fortification of the Canal Zone became a matter of dispute between them, but in the end 16" guns were installed in the hillsides, and the Pacific locks were located well inland, beyond the reach of naval gunfire. The security of Panama, and thus the politics of Central America, has been of sensitive concern to the United States right up to the present day.

Plate 21.

PREUSSEN

Kiel Canal, 1905

For many years the German General Staff worried about the spectacle of war on two fronts. As a principal remedy the railway system was improved across Germany, but in the event of such a war, the navy had an even more serious impediment: the Danish peninsula of Jutland that divides the Baltic from the North Sea. In 1887 work started on cutting a canal across the base of the peninsula, from Kiel on the Baltic to the mouth of the Elbe River above Hamburg. Eight years later the 60-mile long Kaiser Wilhelm Canal

was complete, and its locks were capable of lifting the largest battleships securely and secretly from one sea to the other. The passage cut out two hundred miles.

The picture shows the new battleship *Preussen*, one of the last of the pre-Dreadnoughts, passing through the freshly opened canal in 1905.

The appearance of *Dreadnought* in 1906 all at once made *Preussen* obsolete. Germany faced the prospect of replacing the battle fleet with Dreadnoughts, and this meant

ships so much larger and deeper in draft that they would be unable to negotiate the canal.

Without hesitation, Germany embarked on the construction of a fleet of new battleships uninhibited by considerations of size. At the same time the country began the immense task of reconstructing its vital strategic waterway, including new bridges and locks. By August 1914 the task was complete.

CHAPTER V

THE BATTLE OF THE STRAIT OF TSUSHIMA

Japan had long sustained an effort to keep aloof from external influences before Commodore Perry's visit in 1852. During the last quarter of the nineteenth century, however, she decided to assert herself in the region.

Russia was not alone in regarding Japan's affectation with hauteur. The clash between the two countries marked the end of the rising tide of European power in East Asia and the beginning of a century that has seen a dramatic swing of vitality from west to east.

During the first year of the Russo-Japanese War (1904-1905), several naval engagements took place off Port Arthur in Manchuria, in the course of which the Japanese established an ascendancy. The government in St. Petersburg decided to send the Baltic Fleet to reinforce the Russian squadron blockaded in Port Arthur. Its voyage halfway around the world became an epic, but the great naval battle fought off the coast of Japan ended in crushing defeat. Czarist Russia never recovered from this blow to its power and prestige. Britain, which was the mentor of the Japanese navy and supplier of its ships, was deeply impressed. Allied to Japan by treaty, she withdrew her battleship strength from Eastern waters for 40 years, and Japan entered the rank of world powers, hitherto occupied exclusively by Europeans.

The senility and decline of the once mighty Chinese Empire provided the background to the Russo-Japanese War. Many foreign nations saw in the decline of China an opportunity to gain access to new markets, and countries scrambled to obtain territorial concessions up and down the coast. Japan went further, and in a brief but bloody war from 1894 to 1895, she obtained control of the island of Formosa and of a nominally independent Korea, plus the Liaodong Peninsula in Manchuria.

The latter acquisition aroused the envy of Russia, who badly wanted an ice-free port in the Far East. With the support of Germany and France, the Russians were able to frustrate the Japanese, and themselves first seized and then obtained a lease of the Manchurian peninsula. Thereupon Russia extended the Trans-Siberian Railway southward to this point and built a naval base that they called Port Arthur.

Japan determined to recover her prize, but in order to transport her armies to Korea without interference, she needed to create a navy strong enough to tackle the Russian fleet in the East.

Steadily and deliberately, the Japanese Navy was built up by placing orders with foreign shipyards, mainly in Britain, and the fleet was methodically trained for war.

Russia, by contrast, was supremely complacent. The Russian Navy judged that its forces stationed in Vladivostok and Port Arthur were entirely capable of preventing Japanese troop landings. The Russians took a lofty view of the idea that an Eastern race could possibly wage modern war effectively.

Japan struck first. Without a declaration of war, Japanese torpedo boats were sent to destroy the Russian warships in Port Arthur. Two battleships were damaged, eliminating the Russian superiority in numbers.

The war became a long-drawn blockade; while the

Plate 22.

DREADNOUGHT

St. John's, Antigua, 1906

Soon after her completion in September 1906, the revolutionary new battleship *Dreadnought* was sent on trials before taking up duty as flagship of the Home Fleet. Her shakedown cruise took her to the Mediterranean and to the West Indies; in the course of it, she covered 7,000 miles at an average of 17.5 knots. She was the first large warship to be powered by turbines, and such sustained high performance was cause for astonishment. The most striking innovation, however, was her all-big-gun armament of ten 12" guns all mounted in turrets.

The tramp steamer loading sugar in the background of the picture is emblematic of the worldwide spread of British shipping. Antigua had been well placed to windward in the days of sail as a fleet base for control of both Greater and Lesser Antilles, and though Nelson's English Harbour was too small for the age of steam, the capital, St. Johns, was still a regular port of call for the Royal Navy. That has not changed; in 1987 the sinister outline of a nuclear-powered submarine could be seen in the same anchorage, lying beside multi-decked, diesel-engined cruise liners.

Dreadnought is flying her recognition signal, "Battleship 01," and the instruction, "Send an officer to take orders."

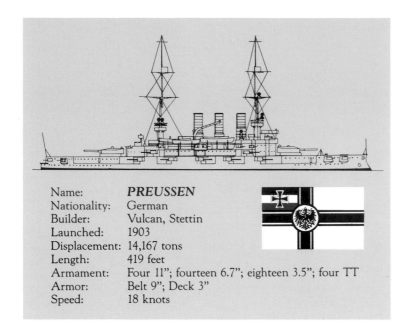

Name: **PREUSSEN**
Nationality: German
Builder: Vulcan, Stettin
Launched: 1903
Displacement: 14,167 tons
Length: 419 feet
Armament: Four 11"; fourteen 6.7"; eighteen 3.5"; four TT
Armor: Belt 9"; Deck 3"
Speed: 18 knots

Japanese were the ones to sow mines in the harbor entrance. The energetic Russian Admiral Makarov was killed when his flagship detonated a mine and sank with all hands after a frightful explosion.

Then it was the Japanese turn for a shock. Goaded by the Japanese success, the Russians high-handedly laid mines outside territorial waters. Two Japanese battleships maneuvering off the port struck mines in the open sea and were sunk with serious loss of life. This was a heavy blow, for the island nation had no distant fleets to call upon for reinforcements.

Makarov's successor, Vitjevt, was a man of lesser clay. Even with renewed Russian superiority in heavy ships, he still seemed irresolute. Nevertheless, his final sortie in August 1904, as the Japanese army was closing in on Port Arthur after six months of fighting, looked close to achieving a breakout to Vladivostok. The Japanese commander, Admiral Togo, who had a slight edge in speed, was able to keep the range open, but even so his ships were hit repeatedly by the excellent Russian shooting, and he had insufficient margin to be able to head them off. His flagship *Mikasa* received heavy punishment,

Japanese freely transported their armies across the Yellow Sea and steadily converged on the fortifications of Port Arthur, the Russian ships, secure in the protected anchorage, made only reluctant sorties.

There were some nasty surprises. While the Russians had been first in the world to use underwater mines during the Crimean War 50 years earlier, the

**Rozhestvensky's voyage
October 1904 to May 1905**

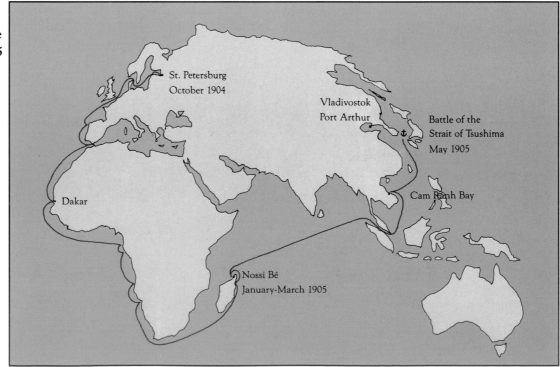

and it seemed only a matter of time before some vital part of the ship would be affected.

Two lucky shots decided the day. The Russian flagship *Tzarevitch* was hit on the bridge and on the conning tower, killing Vitjevt and jamming the helm. Confusion overtook the Russian line. One ship tried gallantly to ram *Mikasa*, but assailed by a torrent of Japanese shellfire, the Russians retired to the protection of their shore batteries. *Tzarevitch* and three light cruisers made a dash for the open sea, but they were too badly damaged to reach Vladivostok and were obliged to seek refuge in neutral Chinese ports.

The Russian ships never emerged again. Bottled up in the harbor, they were sunk one by one as heavy howitzers found their range. Plunging fire from these land-based weapons proved capable of penetrating armored decks and caused mortal injury to the Russian battleships. In January 1905 the garrison surrendered.

The second phase of the war was still to come. In June officials in St. Petersburg decided to send the Baltic Fleet to raise the siege of Port Arthur. It was a bold enterprise, many would say foolhardy.

Admiral Rozhestvensky, who was appointed to command the force, faced a prodigious task. No Russian fleet had been trained and equipped for operations on the high seas far from home base. The creaking bureaucracy of Czarist Russia frustrated all endeavors to instill some sense of urgency to the arming and provisioning of such a force. Crews were ill trained, and large numbers of the men were disaffected with the regime and with the war. The regular navy personnel had been mostly posted to the Far East; those who remained were untrained conscripts or old men whose seamanship was out of date.

The ships comprising what was termed the Second Pacific Squadron were also a motley crew. There were four brand new battleships of the *Suvoroff* class, which were built in St. Petersburg but modeled on the *Tzarevitch* of French design. Little discipline had been exerted in limiting additions to the designed displacement of the battleships, with the result that they sat low in the water, stability was impaired, and their armored belts were largely submerged.

In addition to this group, there was one other fairly modern battleship (the sister of two at Port Arthur) and two slow old ironclads. The cruisers present consisted of two modern 6"-gun ships and two fast light cruisers, plus an elderly armored cruiser that had only recently discarded its square-sail rig, and there was a flotilla of nine torpedo-boat destroyers. The squadron was supported by 20 auxiliaries of different kinds and sizes, including a hospital ship and a repair vessel. Reciprocating engines of the day were notoriously unreliable.

By far the most serious problem facing the dogged Rozhestvensky was that of bunkering. Port Arthur lay 18,000 miles from Kronshtadt. (The battleships drew too much water to pass through the Suez Canal.) His fleet of 40 ships consumed 3,000 tons of coal a day; together they needed half a million tons to reach their destination.

Britain was hostile. Coaling stations in the British Empire were denied to the Russian ships. The French were equivocal. All kinds of efforts were made to ensure supplies en route. Finally, the Russians entered a contract with the Hamburg-Amerika Line, who made 60 colliers available to supply the ships along the way.

But this was not enough. There were gaps in the chain of available anchorages. The ships had to cram on coal in every available space, including in companionways, on deck, even piled in officers' cabins. The crossing of the Indian Ocean was to be managed by coaling at sea. The experts smiled. Regarded as hopelessly impractical, coaling at sea was an undertaking so arduous and slow that it was only done as a last resort, but Rozhestvensky was determined.

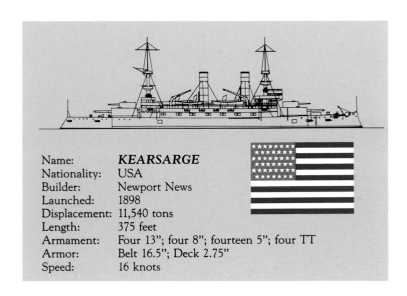

Name: **KEARSARGE**
Nationality: USA
Builder: Newport News
Launched: 1898
Displacement: 11,540 tons
Length: 375 feet
Armament: Four 13"; four 8"; fourteen 5"; four TT
Armor: Belt 16.5"; Deck 2.75"
Speed: 16 knots

Plate 23.

KEARSARGE

Portsmouth, New Hampshire, 1906

Kearsarge shown in the dry dock at Portsmouth Navy Yard, New Hampshire. Completed in 1900, *Kearsarge* and her sister ship *Kentucky* pioneered the use of superimposed guns, 8" above 13", in the same turrets. This disposition was followed by the later *Virginia* class, but at the time it was the subject of much controversy within the Navy. The layout provided all eight guns with wide arcs of fire, but it made the armament vulnerable to severe loss from a single hit, and the additional weight topside had ill effects on stability.

In common with many American battleships, *Kearsarge* and *Kentucky* were equipped with cage masts in 1910, and at the same time their bridge structures were cut down to reduce the risk of debris interfering with the armored conning tower in the event of action damage.

Kearsarge was the only American battleship not named for a state. Her namesake was the Union screw frigate that sank the Confederate *Alabama* off Cherbourg, France, during the Civil War.

One of the ship's bilge keels can be seen following the lower curve of the hull. The ensign flying at the stern indicates that the battleship is still in commission.

Threatened and coerced into some kind of sailing order by its unflagging commander, the heterogeneous armada finally steamed unsteadily out of the Baltic Sea on October 16, 1904. It was accompanied by the inevitable foul-smelling cloud of brown-black coal smoke.

The progress of the Russian fleet to eastern waters was a nightmare, starting in the North Sea, when the Russian crews imagined they were being attacked at night by Japanese torpedo boats. The Russians opened fire, sinking a British fishing trawler and setting three others on fire. Abject apologies scarcely mollified the British, who came to the brink of war. The incident was one of the first cases to be referred to the International Court of Justice at the Hague.

En route, diplomatic wrangles took place at every port they put into for coaling. Elderly warships were plagued by breakdowns, and elderly commanders were beset by incompetence.

Plate 24.

LOUISIANA

Suez, 1909

Ever since the American acquisition of the Philippines, the U.S. Navy was faced with the possibility of having to conduct a campaign on the further side of the Pacific, twice the extent of the Atlantic Ocean.

In 1907 President Theodore Roosevelt sent the newly created battle fleet around the world as a demonstration of America's naval capability. Sixteen battleships sailed from Hampton Roads, Virginia, in December 1907. The ships were painted white with buff-colored upperworks and funnels, and they became known by the press as the Great White Fleet.

Calling at South American ports, the coal-burning battleships made their way around Cape Horn to San Francisco. They visited Hawaii, Samoa, New Zealand, Australia, the Philippines, Japan, and China and returned home via the South China Sea, the Indian Ocean, the Red Sea, the Mediterranean, and the Atlantic. Less than three years had elapsed since the disastrous experience of the Russian Baltic fleet sent around the world to Tsushima; the significance of the far more powerful American operation was not lost upon observers.

Louisiana is portrayed entering the southern end of the Suez Canal on one of the last stages of the 14-month voyage. Opened in 1867, Suez was of no less importance to Britain for naval deployment than it was for her commerce, and the canal was still regarded as of vital concern in 1956.

Plate 25.

AGAMEMNON

Gibraltar, 1911

The pre-Dreadnought battleship *Agamemnon* approaches Gibraltar in 1911. She is an interesting transitional design, going some way towards the concept of the Dreadnought type with its all-big-gun armament. Her main armament consists of 14 heavy guns—four 12" caliber and ten 9.2" caliber—in eight turrets.

Comparison can be made with the new Dreadnought battleship *St. Vincent* lying ahead of her and the Dreadnought cruiser *Invincible* tied up alongside the mole. Both ships carry an all-big-gun armament of 12" guns.

Agamemnon, appropriately, fought near the site of Troy. During an attempt to force the passage of the Dardanelles, she was fired upon from a Turkish fort and struck by a 14"-round stone shot, which was retained on board as a curiosity. She shot down a Zeppelin over Salonika, and in due course the Turkish armistice was signed on her quarterdeck.

The naval historian Richard Hough describes the process of coaling at Dakar:

> With oakum or damp cotton waste stuffed into their mouths, the thermometer at 120 degrees and the humidity in the nineties, the crews set to work. Soon a black cloud rose and enveloped every warship and its attendant collier; and from the shore the harbour appeared to be filled with smouldering hulks. The sun looked like an orange ball from the decks of the men-of-war; while from the depths of the colliers' holds, where the men choked and coughed and sweated under their filthy black loads, it looked like a tiny, blood-red spot. When from time to time a man fainted, a bucket of water was thrown over him, and when he came round he picked up his fallen sack or basket and went on with his work. The coaling continued without a pause, and it took over twenty-nine hours to empty the colliers' holds.[3]

At Madagascar the coaling company broke off its contract with Russia. While the fleet lay sweating in the steamy tropical heat of Nossi Bé, the ships received news of the fall of Port Arthur. News also filtered through to the lower decks of riots in St. Petersburg and of the massacre at the Winter Palace.

The Russian sailors fell sick to tropical diseases, and few escaped the general atmosphere of demoralization. Mess decks were crowded and unhealthy, provisioning had been inadequate, and discipline was erratic. Mutiny broke out, and on two occasions the flagship's guns had to be trained on a unit of her own fleet.

After eight weeks of interminable negotiations, Admiral Rozhestvensky bought the German colliers, using no authority other than his own. Finally he was able once more to raise steam and set off resolutely across the Indian Ocean. As the ships passed through the Strait of Malacca, the stirring news was telegraphed around the world. A foot of

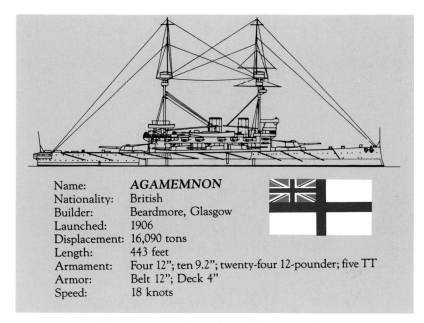

Name:	**AGAMEMNON**
Nationality:	British
Builder:	Beardmore, Glasgow
Launched:	1906
Displacement:	16,090 tons
Length:	443 feet
Armament:	Four 12"; ten 9.2"; twenty-four 12-pounder; five TT
Armor:	Belt 12"; Deck 4"
Speed:	18 knots

green weed was seen trailing from their waterlines after their long stay in tropical waters.

The Russian Admiral was saddled with yet another imposition. Over strenuous protests he was ordered to take under his command a further contingent of ships. Ancient, slow, and unbattleworthy, the collection of coast-defense vessels had been sent out via the Suez Canal and had caught up with him in Indo-China. They added nothing to his fighting strength, and they further reduced the collective speed of the fleet.

The point of rendezvous was Cam Ranh Bay, a base later used by Japanese warships in the Second World War, by American ships engaged in Vietnam, and in modern times once more by the Russians.

On the trip to Cam Ranh Bay, Admiral Rozhestvensky's second in command, Felkersam, died of a stroke. So near to battle, Rozhestvensky decided that the news must be suppressed, and the Admiral's flag was not hauled down.

In the meantime the Japanese commander Admiral Togo had had ample time in which to make his preparations. He had spent six months on refitting and bringing his ships and their crews to a well-

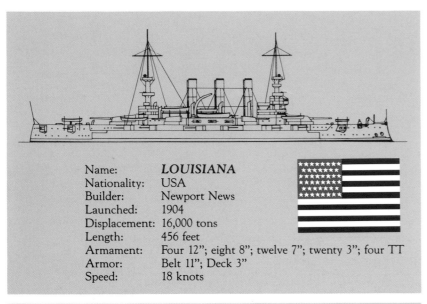

Name:	**LOUISIANA**
Nationality:	USA
Builder:	Newport News
Launched:	1904
Displacement:	16,000 tons
Length:	456 feet
Armament:	Four 12"; eight 8"; twelve 7"; twenty 3"; four TT
Armor:	Belt 11"; Deck 3"
Speed:	18 knots

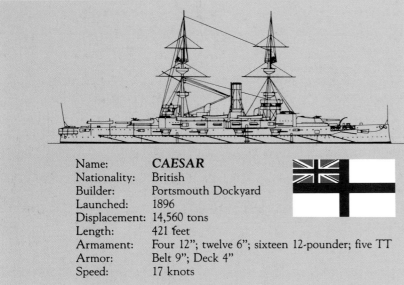

Name:	**CAESAR**
Nationality:	British
Builder:	Portsmouth Dockyard
Launched:	1896
Displacement:	14,560 tons
Length:	421 feet
Armament:	Four 12"; twelve 6"; sixteen 12-pounder; five TT
Armor:	Belt 9"; Deck 4"
Speed:	17 knots

disciplined state of readiness. A squadron of armed merchantmen, each equipped with wireless, was assigned to act as scouts. The Japanese were again outnumbered in battleships, for they still had only four, but eight powerful 8"-gun armored cruisers under Admiral Kamimura were added to extend the battle line. Their cruiser force also included four

fast light cruisers under Admiral Dewa. Nevertheless, Togo was seriously outgunned.

Togo's strengths included an 8-knot advantage in speed, his well-drilled veteran crews, and his perception of the Russian weakness in maneuver. Through the morning mist of May 29, Rozhestvensky's ships panted northwards under their trailing cloud of smoke. They emerged from the passage of the Strait of Tsushima in line ahead, pitching and rolling in the rising sea. The Russian fleet had been reported at dawn, and it was shadowed all the way by Dewa's cruisers.

At noon the Russian Admiral ordered a 90-degree turn to starboard in succession. Could it have been his intention to form his ships into line abreast? From such a formation a simultaneous turn to one side or the other would have laid his ships broadside across the enemy's path. This was the classic naval maneuver: "Crossing the Enemy's T." The technique would bring the broadside armament of the whole fleet to bear on just the leading ships of the enemy line, while the guns of the others were masked.

Ten years later at the Battle of Jutland, Admiral Jellicoe was faced with a similar quandary: which way to turn so that when the unseen enemy swept into view, his fleet would be deployed across their path.

Whatever Rozhestvensky's intentions, when only his four leading ships had made the turn, more of Togo's ships appeared to the northwest. If this were to prove to be the main force, the Russian turn to the east was wrong. So Rozhestvensky canceled the order and returned to the old course; his First Division now formed a line parallel to the Second but somewhat ahead.

Togo materialized at 1:40 p.m. with the main Japanese battle fleet bearing down from the northeast. While still out of range, he cut across the bows of the Russians to place himself on their port bow and then executed a 180-degree turn, placing his flagship ahead of the Russians on a slightly converging course. The Japanese were badly exposed at the moment of their turn, as each unit in succession passed through the same spot, but the Russians were engaged in trying to reform in single line ahead, and their ships became bunched together in the process.

Nevertheless, the Russian fire was uncomfortably accurate. Shooting from a range of 6,500 yards, many hits were scored against the Japanese. *Mikasa*, in the van, suffered badly as before, and Togo was slightly wounded as he stood impassively on the open bridgework. Two armored cruisers were forced to leave the line, including a ship called *Asama* (of which more will be heard later).

Now it was the turn of the Japanese. Steadily drawing out of view of the Russian rear, they concentrated their fire on the flagships of the First and Second Divisions. Gradually drawing ahead they turned little by little to starboard, closing the range. Rozhestvensky, penned inside his armored conning tower, seems to have been gripped by a kind of inertia after all these months of passionate endeavor to bring his fleet so far.

While there was still a chance for him to seize the initiative, to swing to port across the Japanese rear, he allowed his flagship instead to be pushed further and further to starboard. His last opportunity slipped past.

The range between the fleets dropped to less than 5,000 yards, and guns of all calibers—12", 10", and 6"—were firing indiscriminately. Spotting the fall of shot in such a welter of splashes became completely impossible.

A British observer reported afterwards that Japanese gunnery improved as the primitive system of fire control was drowned in the noise and confusion of battle. Reduction of range, he wrote dryly, had much to do with increased accuracy, but the shooting improved progressively as the method of determining the range was frustrated by the confusion of battle.

The Japanese initially used shimose powder, a newly developed explosive, and less sensitive fuses which ensured penetration of hulls or upperworks before detonation of the shell. The widespread but superficial destruction and injuries caused by high-explosive shell quickly reduced the fighting effectiveness of the Russian crews. After 2:30 the Japanese switched to armor-piercing projectiles.

At 2:50, an hour after the main battle had commenced, *Oslyabya*, flagship of the Russian Second Division, staggered out of line and stopped, the target of Kamimura's armored cruisers. Thirty minutes later she settled by the head, capsized, and finally sank bottom upwards. She was the first armored ship ever to be sunk by gunfire at sea.

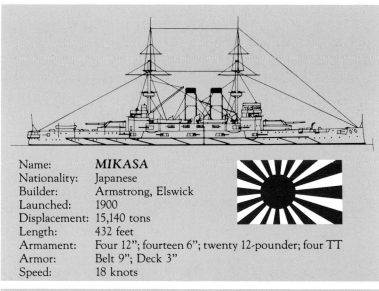

Name:	**MIKASA**
Nationality:	Japanese
Builder:	Armstrong, Elswick
Launched:	1900
Displacement:	15,140 tons
Length:	432 feet
Armament:	Four 12"; fourteen 6"; twenty 12-pounder; four TT
Armor:	Belt 9"; Deck 3"
Speed:	18 knots

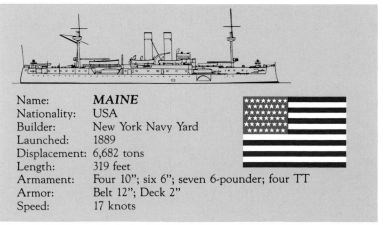

Name:	**MAINE**
Nationality:	USA
Builder:	New York Navy Yard
Launched:	1889
Displacement:	6,682 tons
Length:	319 feet
Armament:	Four 10"; six 6"; seven 6-pounder; four TT
Armor:	Belt 12"; Deck 2"
Speed:	17 knots

Plate 26.

THUNDERER and CONQUEROR

Plymouth, 1912

Two Dreadnoughts are seen just after emerging from the Hamoaze into Plymouth Sound. Behind *Thunderer* lies Drake's Island with the seaward breakwater in the distance. In the foreground is a splendid Victorian cast-iron pleasure pier, which stood at the foot of Plymouth Hoe until it was destroyed by bombs in 1941. The two ships are navigating the Smeaton Channel, first blasted during construction of the Eddystone Lighthouse. The channel is a tricky passage. Big ships must follow the Cornish shore before doubling back close in to the Hoe and then swinging out into the Sound.

Thunderer, the last big warship to be built at Blackwall on the Thames, was the first type to mount the new 13.5" gun. Her massive tripod mast was stepped aft of the forefunnel, whose heat and fumes would tend to kipper the unfortunate gunnery officer stationed in the foretop. On board *Thunderer* in 1912, nevertheless, trials proved conclusively the superiority of centralized director control of the guns.

Rozhestvensky's flagship *Suvoroff* had also taken heavy punishment; her hull was holed, and the after turret and funnels were destroyed. At 2:55 she veered out of control, her helm jammed hard to starboard. *Suvoroff*'s masts and signaling halyards were shot away. The Admiral lay wounded and unconscious; the Russian fleet was without command.

After this point the battle degenerated into a massacre. The Russians fought courageously in circumstances without hope.

Japanese ships, closing to within a mile of their quarry, doubled backwards and forwards to head off each attempt at escape. The remaining Russian ships received a fearful cannonade. Half an hour later *Alexander III* was disabled and obliged to draw out of line, burning furiously. The scene became more and more confused, as smoke from funnels and fires spread wider and mingled with the mist.

The Russians fought back spiritedly all afternoon. Togo sent in his destroyers, while he hauled the battle fleet away to the north to repair damage and recuperate.

Rozhestvensky was transferred, unconscious, from the drifting wreck of his flagship to a torpedo boat. *Suvoroff* nevertheless fought on heroically for many hours. Long after dark the smoking hulk eventually foundered after being struck by four torpedoes. There were no survivors.

At 6:00 Togo returned to the south, and the slaughter was renewed. The Russian ships were making their way once more to the north. Fires on *Alexander III* broke out afresh, and a huge hole was torn in her side. At 7:00 she ran up a signal of distress, abruptly hauled out of line, and turned turtle. She took down with her almost the entire ship's company of 800.

The sun set shortly after 6:30, and Togo determined not to risk his precious ships to the hazards of a night action. By 7:20 he ceased firing and led his battle squadron away to the north. The last salvo of the day produced the most sensational effect; the battleship *Borodino* was already badly on fire when a shell evidently penetrated directly to her magazines. The stricken ship disappeared in an immense cloud of steam and smoke shot through with shafts of flame.

During the hours of darkness, Japanese torpedo boats fell upon the disorganized remainder of the Russian fleet, pressing home their attacks amidst rising seas. At daylight the survivors, hopelessly outnumbered and surrounded, surrendered to prevent further needless loss of life. *Oryol* was the only modern Russian battleship still afloat.

One cruiser and two destroyers escaped to bring news of the Russian defeat to Vladivostok. Three other cruisers took refuge in neutral ports. Still unconscious, the unfortunate Rozhestvensky fell into the hands of the enemy, when the torpedo boat to which he had been transferred surrendered. The Russians suffered 4,800 dead; 2,000 missing; and 6,000 made prisoner.

"The world stood amazed."[4]

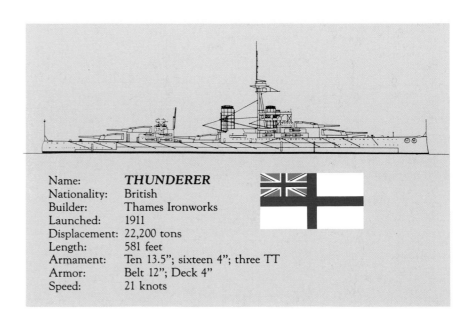

Name:	***THUNDERER***
Nationality:	British
Builder:	Thames Ironworks
Launched:	1911
Displacement:	22,200 tons
Length:	581 feet
Armament:	Ten 13.5"; sixteen 4"; three TT
Armor:	Belt 12"; Deck 4"
Speed:	21 knots

CHAPTER VI

FEAR GOD AND
DREAD NOUGHT

By the end of the nineteenth century, the design of battleships had settled down to a universal pattern, represented by the 27 ships built for the Royal Navy between 1898 and 1904. They had displacements in the region of 15,000 tons, and they mounted four 12" guns in two twin turrets, forward and aft on the center line, with a secondary armament of twelve 6" in casemates along the sides. Such ships were protected by a 6" to 9" belt of Krupp face-hardened steel armor along the waterline over the vital central area of the hull, plus a 2" armored deck below water level to protect the engine room and magazines. Vertical reciprocating engines using the triple-expansion principle, and driving twin screws propelled them at 18 knots. Two massive funnels provided the draft for a host of coal-fired boilers, and two tall masts supported spotting tops for gunnery observation, searchlights, semaphores, and signal yards. A large number of 12-pounder and 3-pounder weapons were mounted topsides for dealing with torpedo boats, and the battleships themselves were provided with underwater torpedo tubes. Torpedo nets were carried on booms that could be swung out from the hull as protection from torpedo attack while at anchor.

In 1895 Armstrong introduced its new high-velocity 12" guns employing "smokeless powder." The barrels were of wire-wound construction in place of wrought-iron coils shrunk around a steel tube, enabling the use of the new propellant, cordite, which provided much greater muzzle velocity. Such weapons had a range of 12,000 yards. The chances of scoring a hit were remote, however, for each gun was laid individually, there were no range finders or telescopic sights, and the rate of fire was slow.

The general expectation was that naval battles would be fought at "decisive" range, maybe 3,000 yards. At this distance the quick-firing secondary battery of 6" guns would smash the enemy guns, superstructure, and control positions, while the heavy guns groped for a knockout blow on the waterline.

Some naval men were not content with this doctrine. Captain Percy Scott in the Royal Navy and Lieutenant Commander Sims in the United States found scope for big improvements in gunlaying drill and in the speed of loading, and accuracy was further increased by the introduction of telescopic sights. Gunnery experts discovered that central control of the guns, with the fall of shot being corrected by an officer stationed aloft, enabled consistent hitting at more than 6,000 yards. In order to find the range quickly, only half the guns were fired at one time, so that the interval between corrections could be reduced. Thus evolved the technique of "salvo" firing.

A salvo, to be useful, should consist of more than two rounds, and a mixture of calibers led to hopeless confusion when watching for the splash of shells. The conventional arrangement of four big guns was therefore ill-suited to the demands of increased fighting distances.

Other pressures to increase the range of battle were the growing speed, range, and reliability of torpedoes, which began to make the large armored ship seem less invulnerable and the assumption of

Plate 27.

GOOD HOPE

Table Bay, Cape Town, 1913

The armored cruiser *Good Hope* is being assisted into dock by a South African Railways and Harbours tug. In the background rises Table Mountain and Devil's Peak. The mountain is capped by the famous table-cloth, a white cloud formed by the southeast summer wind that continually dissipates itself as it flows over the north-facing slope like a waterfall. The ship is signalling to the shore station, "I require assistance. I have a Service telegram."

Good Hope was, appropriately enough, posted to the Cape of Good Hope as flagship of the South Atlantic Station, and she is flying the flag of the Rear-Admiral. The naval station of Simonstown lies 25 miles south of Cape Town on the east coast of the Cape Peninsula.

Good Hope is a fine example of the ar-mored cruiser type, 35 of which were built for the Royal Navy between 1900 and 1907. With the appearance in 1907 of the Dread-nought cruiser, or battle cruiser as it became known, the armored cruiser was eclipsed.

At the Battle of Coronel on November 1, 1914, *Good Hope* came to a disastrous end and was sunk with all hands. She was outclassed and outmaneuvered by German Admiral von Spee with his squadron of faster and better-armed ships.

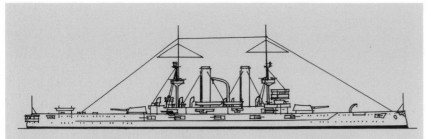

Name:	**TRIUMPH**
Nationality:	British
Builder:	Vickers, Barrow
Launched:	1903
Displacement:	11,985 tons
Length:	479 feet
Armament:	Four 10"; fourteen 7.5"; fourteen 14-pounder; two 12-pounder; two TT
Armor:	Belt 7"; Deck 3"
Speed:	19 knots

close-range action correspondingly more dangerous.

In 1902 Philip Watts, the Chief Naval Architect at the Armstrong yard in Elswick near Newcastle, succeeded Sir William White as Chief Constructor of the Navy. White, the most masterly of Victorian naval architects, had been in the post for 17 years. Several countries were preparing plans for a big step forward in warship design, but Britain, with her great superiority in numbers, was not the most eager to see a major innovation. The first of Watts' designs was an interesting transitional type, *Lord Nelson* and *Agamemnon*, constrained in size by strict Admiralty instructions to enable them to use existing dry docks. These ships carried a mixed main armament of 14 guns—four 12" and ten 9.2"—all of which were mounted in turrets, and they incorporated greatly improved underwater protection.

The key personality in the design revolution was Admiral Sir John Fisher, a naval officer who had a dynamic career. Outspoken, iconoclastic, and technically minded, he swept aside traditional attitudes and aroused violent antagonism as well as

Plate 28.
TRIUMPH
Hong Kong, 1913

Longer and slimmer than other British battleships, *Triumph* and *Swiftsure* were quite distinctive, even exotic in appearance. They had been designed for the Chilean navy and constructed in England, but they were purchased by the Royal Navy on completion in 1904 in order to prevent their being sold elsewhere (most likely Russia).

Their architect was Sir Edward Reed, erstwhile Director of Naval Construction and designer of *Devastation*, and their particulars were impressive. Intended to counter six fast armored cruisers acquired by Argentina, the battleships were the first to exceed 20 knots, and their heavy armament would have made them masters of the Argentine ships.

Triumph was flagship on the China Station in 1914. She led the attack on the German base at Tsingtao in China and later took part in operations against Turkey, trying to breach the Dardanelles. She was sunk by a German submarine while engaged in shore bombardment off Gallipoli. The Australian troops ashore missed her support and even subscribed funds in an attempt to have her raised.

In the picture the harbor at Hong Kong is crowded with shipping, including *Tamar*, an old troopship that was roofed over and lay in the roadstead as an accommodation ship. Also identifiable are *Minotaur*, a British armored cruiser, which with her sister *Defence* was stationed at Hong Kong from 1910 to 1914, and her German counterpart *Scharnhorst*, which with *Gneisenau* was stationed at Tsingtao. Another visitor, the enormous French cruiser *Montcalm*, is partly visible on the left.

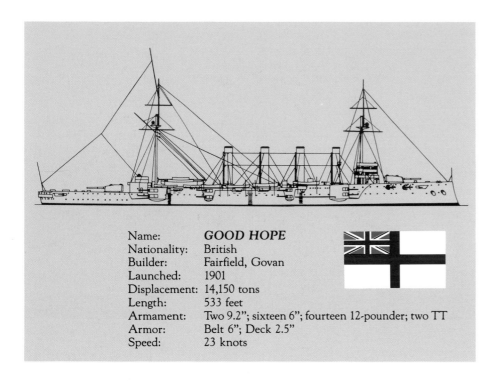

Name: **GOOD HOPE**
Nationality: British
Builder: Fairfield, Govan
Launched: 1901
Displacement: 14,150 tons
Length: 533 feet
Armament: Two 9.2"; sixteen 6"; fourteen 12-pounder; two TT
Armor: Belt 6"; Deck 2.5"
Speed: 23 knots

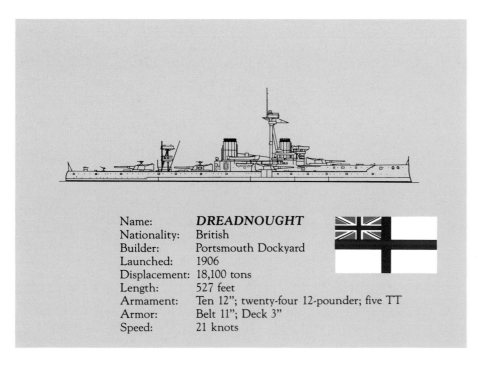

Name: **DREADNOUGHT**
Nationality: British
Builder: Portsmouth Dockyard
Launched: 1906
Displacement: 18,100 tons
Length: 527 feet
Armament: Ten 12"; twenty-four 12-pounder; five TT
Armor: Belt 11"; Deck 3"
Speed: 21 knots

passionate advocates of reform. During his term as Commander-in-Chief in the Mediterranean, "Jackie" Fisher had floated ideas for new types of warships, and technical studies were worked out by William Gard, the Chief Constructor at Malta dockyard. When the Admiral moved to Portsmouth, Gard was also transferred, and in 1905 Fisher was promoted to First Sea Lord.

In January he convened a Committee on Designs. The formidable membership included Watts, Jellicoe, Battenberg, and Gard. Shipbuilders, engineers, naval officers, and an eminent scientist, Lord Kelvin, were also in the group. Their concern focused on the ability to bring a greater weight of fire power to bear on one part of an enemy line, simplicity of fire control, and speed. Fisher's dictum was that the battleship was the embodiment of the concentration of gunpower. It took the committee only seven weeks to settle on the design.

In May 1905 the Battle of Tsushima occurred. A small advantage in speed had given the Japanese the tactical initiative, enabling them to concentrate the fire of all their ships on one part of the enemy's line. The Russians had never been able to bring the full strength of their firepower to bear.

Additionally, the ships had proved extraordinarily resistant. In spite of terrible damage to funnels and upperworks, the Russian armored ships survived for hours; only the biggest guns proved capable of inflicting a fatal blow.

All at once it seemed self-evident. If the issue could be settled by big guns alone, logic demanded the all-big-gun ship.

The idea was not new; Italian designer Cuniberti had advocated it, Watts had gone part of the way toward achieving it with *Lord Nelson*, the United States had decided to build all-big-gun ships, and the Japanese had already started construction on two. The Royal Navy was obliged to face the fact that the world's greatest navy was about to be outclassed.

Four months after Tsushima, the keel of Fisher's new ship was laid at Portsmouth Dockyard. Construction time was cut by simplification and standardization of parts. The same philosophy that had led to a single type of gun and size of ammunition was applied to the structure of the ship. It was the speed with which she materialized, as much as her radical design, that caused such a sensation; within less than a year, *Dreadnought* was steaming out to sea between the South Railway Jetty and Camper & Nicholson's Gosport yard.

The name selected for the ship was both traditional to the Royal Navy and appropriate. When he was subsequently elevated to the peerage, Fisher chose as his motto, "Fear God and Dread Nought."

What made her so remarkable? *Dreadnought*'s formidability lay not in any one quality but in the combination. She was larger, faster, better protected, and incomparably more heavily gunned than any previous battleship. She mounted ten 12" guns in five turrets in place of the customary two, but after this she had no secondary guns, only 12-pounders for protection against torpedo boats. Equally importantly, she was the first to make use of the turbine. So far only a light cruiser and some smaller craft had been powered by the rotary steam engine so recently developed by Charles Parsons, but the great new Cunarders were quickly to follow suit. *Dreadnought*'s engines gave her a margin of 3 knots in speed over existing battleships, and they did so with tireless reliability in striking contrast to the old.

Dreadnought burst upon the naval world. Suddenly all other battleships looked out of date, and every naval power was obliged to reappraise the strength of its fleet. She precipitated a furious shipbuilding race to achieve, or to retain, maritime supremacy. To distinguish the new battleships from inferior types, they were all described as Dreadnoughts.

In the eight years leading up to the outbreak of war in 1914, 30 more Dreadnoughts were built for

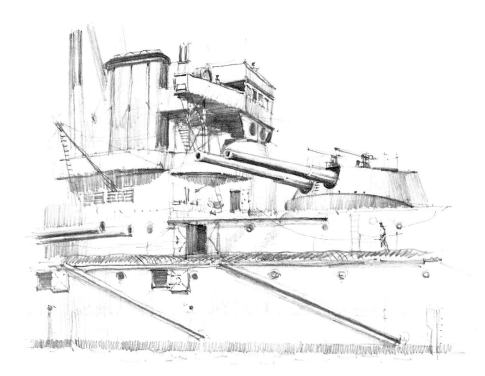

the Royal Navy, 20 for the Germans, and some 40 for other navies. Yet because of the size and cost of such ships, as well as the resources that were needed to man them and put them to sea, in all the world not more than 176 Dreadnought battleships and battle cruisers were built over a period of 40 years. Dozens more were started, but they failed to reach completion.

Dreadnoughts became tokens of power, symbolic of national resolve or of aggressive intentions. A mere handful of Dreadnoughts exerted a major influence on the sway of power in two world wars, and it was only after 1941 that their importance withered away. The last Dreadnought to be built, also British, was named *Vanguard*, and she was completed in 1946. Britain's last battleship never fired a shot in anger, and she was retired in 1960. Alone amongst nations the United States has not yet discarded all of hers.

Plate 29.

HOHENZOLLERN and
FRIEDRICH DER GROSSE
Corfu, April 1914

The Empress Elisabeth of Austria built a palace at Gastóurion, a few miles south of the town of Corfu on the east coast of the Greek Ionian island. "I want a palace with pillared colonnades and hanging gardens— a palace worthy of Achilles, who despised all mortals and did not fear the gods," wrote the Empress.

The Achilleion Palace was bought by Kaiser Wilhelm II in 1907. He used to spend a month there every year, and the whole court moved with him from Berlin. He would sail from Wilhelmshaven in the magnificent Imperial Yacht *Hohenzollern*, accompanied by a suitably impressive naval escort. The Kaiser disembarked at a private jetty, which was linked to the estate by a stone bridge across the public highway. An immense bronze statue of Achilles still stands on the terrace before the house, but the inscription "To the greatest of the Greeks from the greatest of the Germans" has been removed.

The battleship *Friedrich der Grosse* hoisted the flag of the Commander-in-Chief on her commissioning in 1912, and she remained flagship of the High Seas Fleet until 1917. She is anchored on the right of the picture.

The Kaiser's admiration for Greek civilization was equalled only by his enthusiasm for the navy. In June of the same year, he was again aboard *Hohenzollern* for the Kiel Week regatta and the international celebrations to mark the opening of the widened Kaiser Wilhelm Canal. He was on board his racing yacht *Meteor* when news reached him of the assassination of Archduke Ferdinand at Sarajevo.

CHAPTER VII
THE GOEBEN AFFAIR

Invisible strands of alliances and secret understandings entangled the Powers of Europe in a net, and during the summer of 1914 they seemed to stumble with awful inevitability towards a European war. France, bruised by the experience of 1870, had long established her Entente with Russia. The German High Command faced the specter of a war on two fronts. But the alignments were uncertain. Perhaps England would stand aloof? What about Italy? How powerful really was the Russian colossus?

Ottoman Turkey straddled communications between Russia and Western Europe. Senile and corrupt, the despotic Ottoman Empire was disdained by Western politicians, but as the harvest was gathered in across the European continent and the widened locks of the Kiel Canal neared completion, the Kaiser was suddenly struck by the urgency of recruiting Turkey to German arms.

At the same moment the Admiralty in London surveyed the various warships being built in British yards for foreign navies. Only too well aware of the slender British superiority in battleships, they were equally concerned about adding to the naval power of a possible adversary. Two of the ships were Dreadnoughts destined for the Turkish navy: *Reshadieh*, which was just completing steaming trials off Vickers' yard at Barrow-in-Furness, and *Sultan Osman I*, the biggest battleship in the world, which was nearing completion at Elswick. Their Turkish naval crews were already standing by on board a transport in the Tyne when on August 2 the ships

were seized at gunpoint on orders from Whitehall.

The resentment caused by this action may have been just the push needed by the pro-German Enver Bey to get the Grand Vizier, chief minister of the Turkish government, to sign a secret pact with Germany. On August 3 the German Ambassador in Constantinople concluded a flurry of telegrams to Berlin with news of success.

The Turkish government, however, was not a concerted body of men. There were internal rivalries, hesitations, and the tortuous groping for a better deal that often accompanies business in the Middle East. Something more would be needed to make Turkey honor its commitment to the German cause.

What brought Turkey into the war was the passage of the Dardanelles and arrival off Constantinople of the German warships *Goeben* and *Breslau*. Barbara Tuchman, the American historian whose grandfather was then U.S. Ambassador in Constantinople, put it thus: "No other single exploit in the war cast so long a shadow upon the world as the voyage accomplished by Admiral Souchon."[5]

When Turkey joined sides with Germany, the Dardanelles were closed, and Russia's foreign trade dropped to a twentieth of what it had been. Western military support for her became impossible.

Disintegration of the Czarist Empire was hastened, if not precipitated by this event. Bulgaria, Romania, Italy, and Greece were all dragged into the war. Costly and disastrous campaigns were waged against Turkey in Mesopotamia and in trying to force the Dardanelles, leading in their turn to prolongation of the

Plate 30.

GOEBEN and BRESLAU

Constantinople, August 1914

At dawn on Sunday, August 16th, two German warships slipped quietly into the Bosporus and took up moorings below the historic walls of the city of Constantinople. Both ships were still flying the German Imperial ensign. Later in the day at a formal ceremony, the scarlet Turkish flag with star and crescent was raised in its stead, but the command flag of Rear-Admiral Souchon was never hauled down. While the ships were ostensibly sold to Turkey, they remained absolutely in German hands.

Note the broad beam of the battle cruiser Goeben—96 feet compared with 78 feet of the British Invincible—and the anti-torpedo nets that lie bunched along the side of the deck. The louvers, another feature of interest, took the place of traditional goose-necked ventilators serving the engine rooms.

Goeben's two amidships turrets are staggered en échelon (starboard forward of port, contrary to British practice) to enable cross-deck fire on either broadside. Nevertheless, the well-armored secondary battery casemates lie out-

board of the wing turrets. Curiously, the searchlight platforms on the forefunnel are staggered in accordance with the main turrets, and part of the massive funnel cap is tilted asymmetrically to afford them some protection from smoke and cinders.

The slim four-funnelled cruiser Breslau, which can be seen ahead of the flagship, was likewise capable of an impressive top speed of nearly 28 knots.

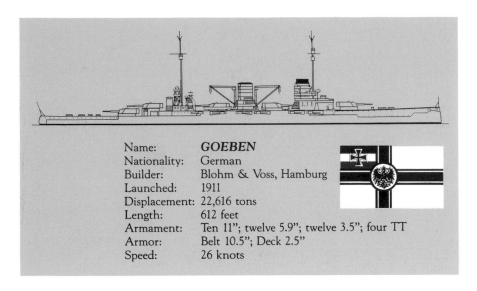

Name: **GOEBEN**
Nationality: German
Builder: Blohm & Voss, Hamburg
Launched: 1911
Displacement: 22,616 tons
Length: 612 feet
Armament: Ten 11"; twelve 5.9"; twelve 3.5"; four TT
Armor: Belt 10.5"; Deck 2.5"
Speed: 26 knots

agony in the trenches of Western Europe. Finally the tottering Ottoman Empire dissolved amidst violent purges of Armenians and Greeks, leaving a legacy of injustice, bitterness, and enmity between ethnic groups throughout the region that continues to this day.

In November 1912 Germany first sent warships to the Mediterranean. The Turks, under pressure from a Bulgarian army at the gates of Constantinople, appealed for an international fleet to uphold the Congress of Berlin. This treaty, signed in 1878, was designed to preserve the international character of the waterway that connects the Black Sea with the Mediterranean by way of the Bosporus, the Sea of Marmara, and the Dardanelles. Ten countries responded. Germany contributed the spanking new battle cruiser *Goeben*, by far the most impressive warship present, accompanied by the light cruiser *Breslau*. Designated the Mediterranean Division, the ships remained after the crisis and were commanded from October 1913 by Rear-Admiral Wilhelm Souchon.

Goeben, the third ship to be built in Germany of the new type of Dreadnought cruiser, was as large as a battleship, fast (27.5 knots on trials), and armed with ten 11" guns.

The Kaiser was delighted at the opportunity to Show the Flag in grand style. The Mediterranean Division toured the length of the inland sea, German funding went to the construction of the Berlin-Baghdad Railway, and a German military mission under General Liman von Sanders struggled to modernize the Turkish Army.

In May 1914 *Goeben* was at Constantinople, where her sailors helped to put out a major fire ashore. From there she paid a call at Beirut and then made her way to Pola at the head of the Adriatic. Souchon had arranged for urgent repairs to *Goeben*'s boilers to be carried out at the Austrian shipyard. The problem was not entirely solved, but she was due to be replaced in October by her sister ship *Moltke*.

On June 28 the heir to the Austrian throne, Archduke Franz Ferdinand, was killed by an assassin in Sarajevo, the capital of Serbia. Following this crime the Austrian demands were extravagant, and on July 28 she declared war on Serbia. The next day Russia commenced mobilization of her army along the Austrian frontier, and on the 30th both powers ordered general mobilization. Souchon cut short repair operations and headed for the mouth of the Adriatic; there was no point in being bottled up.

Germany called upon Russia to demobilize, and then on August 1 she went to war. France, allied by treaty to Russia, announced mobilization. Germany declared war on France on August 3, and the next day she launched an immediate attack by brazenly marching across a corner of Belgium. Germany and Britain had both guaranteed Belgian neutrality. Britain wavered, but she steeled herself to demand German withdrawal from Belgium, failing which she would go to war at midnight on August 4.

It was no surprise to France to find herself again confronting the German army. One of the first priorities on the outbreak of war was to ship three divisions of the Colonial Corps from North Africa to Marseilles. The principal hazard to safe passage

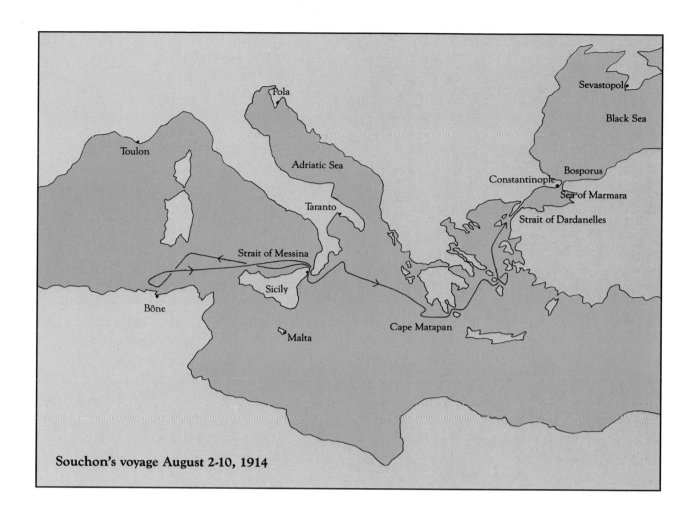

Souchon's voyage August 2-10, 1914

was the German Mediterranean Division.

On August 2 the French government ordered its fleet to sail from Toulon and intercept the German ships before they could interfere with this operation. Admiral Lapeyrère responded in a dilatory manner, getting his ships under way so late and with so little urgency that they arrived off North Africa in dribs and drabs on August 4.

Goeben and *Breslau* were reported passing through the Strait of Messina, located between Sicily and the toe of Italy, in the small hours of August 3, heading west.

The island of Malta lies some 60 miles south of Sicily. The British Mediterranean Fleet, based in Malta, included a squadron of three battle cruisers. As war approached the fleet was given instructions to shadow *Goeben* and to help protect French

troop movements. Admiral Milne, the Commander-in-Chief, also had a squadron of four armored cruisers and four light cruisers under his command. Part of his responsibility was to keep an eye on the much more powerful Austrian fleet, but Austria was not at war with Britain. Italy's intentions were uncertain.

Early on August 3 Milne dispatched two of his battle cruisers, *Indomitable* and *Indefatigable*, westward after the German ships. At 6 p.m. Souchon heard by wireless that Germany was now at war with France, and during the night he received orders from Berlin to proceed at once to Constantinople. He decided nevertheless to startle the French first.

Goeben and *Breslau* bombarded the French Algerian ports of Philippeville and Bône before dawn on August 4, promptly withdrawing the way they had come.

Milne's battle cruisers encountered the German ships at 9:30 a.m.; while not of a friendly nation, the warships belonged to a country with whom Britain was not yet at war.

It must have been a tense moment. No courtesies were echanged, but guns remained trained fore and aft. The British swung round through 180 degrees and took up station astern. Both sides ordered maximum revolutions.

The speed of a coal-fired steamship depends not just on her power and hull design. In some measure it is affected by the extent of barnacle growth on the ship's bottom, the quality of the coal used in the furnaces, and the exertions of her stokers.

All through that blazing August day, the four ships raced through the blue Mediterranean. Gangs of stokers, stripped to the waist and streaked with black, toiled desperately in the glare of the furnaces. The air in the inferno of stokeholds was choked with coal dust raised by the roar of forced-draft fans.

In *Goeben* four men died, scalded by steam bursting from her boiler tubes. Imperceptibly, nevertheless, the warship managed to pull away. Gradually the British battle cruisers dropped back, until by 5 p.m. they were just specks on the horizon.

Being once outstripped makes a lasting impression. Unaware of what the effort had cost their quarry, the British were now convinced that *Goeben* could never be caught in a straight chase.

The British government, anxious to provide no pretext for Italian entry to the war, forbade warships to approach within six miles of the Italian coast. Out of sight of her pursuers, *Goeben* returned to Messina, where she feverishly loaded coal from merchant ships summoned to the rendezvous. The big battle cruiser's appetite was voracious, and her chances of evasion were completely dependent on rapid bunkering. In order to preserve their country's neutrality, the Italians would not allow her to come alongside, so the crew were obliged to shift hundreds of tons without mechanical help. They tore open holes in the decks of the colliers to expedite the process. All through the night they toiled, while the ship's band played and blackened men dropped to the deck in utter exhaustion.

Souchon learned from Berlin of Turkey's vacillation and he decided to stick to the plan to go east. His transmissions were picked up by British ships and divulged his location, but the British were entirely preoccupied with the prospect that Souchon would try to go west in order to fall upon French troop transports or to escape into the Atlantic. They stationed two battle cruisers to the west of the Strait of Messina, leaving only a light cruiser to report on any movement to the east. (The straits are less than three miles wide.)

Souchon emerged to the east of Sicily, dodged north toward the Adriatic in an attempt to evade the watching British cruiser, then turned on his true course toward the southeast.

Milne made no new dispositions. His armored cruisers under Admiral Troubridge, still patroling in the mouth of the Adriatic to keep an eye on the Austrians, were left without specific instructions.

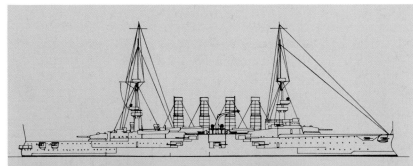

Name:	**SCHARNHORST**
Nationality:	German
Builder:	Blohm & Voss, Hamburg
Launched:	1906
Displacement:	12,781 tons
Length:	475 feet
Armament:	Eight 8.2"; six 5.9"; eighteen 3.5"; four TT
Armor:	Belt 6"; Deck 2"
Speed:	23 knots

Plate 31.

SCHARNHORST and DRESDEN

Beagle Channel, Tierra del Fuego, 1914

Admiral von Spee's Cruiser Squadron based in East Asia crossed the Pacific after the outbreak of war. Arriving off the coast of Chile at the end of October, he inflicted a humiliating defeat on the British at Coronel. Spee's ships vanished, to appear dramatically six weeks later at the Falkland Islands. There they met retribution.

During the period between the two battles, the German squadron rounded Cape Horn. On December 2 the light cruiser *Leipzig* came upon the British four-masted barque *Drummuir*, which was carrying coal to the west coast; she towed her prize into the forbidding but sheltered waters of the Beagle Channel in order to relieve the barque of her cargo.

The surrounding mountains rise in places to 8,000 feet, and the sea passages between them are narrow and treacherous with rocks. Even in summer the region is shrouded in fogs and incessant rain. Charles Darwin called it "a death-like scene of desolation." The big armored cruiser *Scharnhorst* lies on the left, flying the flag of Vice-Admiral Count Maximilian von Spee.

Dresden, on the right, was the only cruiser in the squadron with turbine engines, and this probably enabled her to escape destruction at the Battle of the Falklands. She took refuge in the maze of uncharted channels and islands off the southwest coast of Tierra del Fuego. For more than three months, she furtively eluded her pursuers. *Dresden*, finally cornered by the Royal Navy, scuttled herself at the Juan Fernández Islands, 400 miles west of Valparaiso.

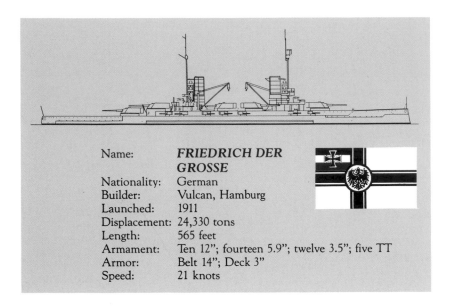

Name:	**FRIEDRICH DER GROSSE**
Nationality:	German
Builder:	Vulcan, Hamburg
Launched:	1911
Displacement:	24,330 tons
Length:	565 feet
Armament:	Ten 12"; fourteen 5.9"; twelve 3.5"; five TT
Armor:	Belt 14"; Deck 3"
Speed:	21 knots

Troubridge moved to intercept. It could have been done. What might have been the outcome, with four armored cruisers pitted against one very much stronger ship and her consort, is impossible to judge. Something like the same balance of forces occurred again in 1939, when three British cruisers in the South Atlantic took on the German pocket battleship *Admiral Graf Spee*.

But Troubridge hesitated. Constrained by orders not to do battle with superior forces, he decided that in a daylight action his cruiser squadron would be inferior to *Goeben* with her long-range guns. Before dawn, therefore, he turned away. He lived to face a court-martial for this decision, and his career was ruined.

The British light cruiser *Gloucester* skillfully resisted determined efforts by *Goeben* and *Breslau* to shake her off and continued her assignment of keeping the enemy ships in sight. Souchon pressed on toward the Aegean, until *Gloucester* was ordered to give up the chase off the southwestern tip of Greece.

Even now, the British could think of no more likely destination for *Goeben* and *Breslau* than the Western Mediterranean. The fleet left Malta in leisurely pursuit to the east.

Souchon, meanwhile, had taken refuge behind one of the countless islands in the Aegean, where he hastily replenished the bunkers from an auxiliary. Sending the collier on to Smyrna, he ordered her to transmit a message to the German Embassy in Constantinople seeking authority to enter the Dardanelles. After an agonizing wait, early on August 10 he received the cryptic instruction: "Enter. Demand surrender of forts. Capture pilot."

Late that afternoon the German warships cautiously closed Cape Helles at the entrance to the historic waterway dividing Europe from Asia. Fortifications encrusted either shore, and the straits were known to be mined. Signal flags fluttered from the halyards: "Require pilot." With decks cleared for action, guns trained on the forts, *Goeben* awaited the interpretation.

A Turkish destroyer emerged, picking her way through the unmarked minefields. In international code she hoisted the laconic message, "Follow me."

The long pale grey battle cruiser, her sides streaked with coal dust and rust after her hectic passage, followed carefully in the wake of the tiny destroyer, screws threshing as she stemmed the swift current in the Dardanelles. They dropped anchor in the Narrows, under the frowning fortress of Chanak.

Enver Bey, Minister for War, had given his own orders for the ships to be allowed in. The Turkish government could come to no decision.

Winston Churchill, expelled from the post of First Lord of the Admiralty after the debacle of Gallipoli, was to write years later that *Goeben* carried "more slaughter, more misery, and more ruin than has ever before been borne within the compass of a ship."

With hindsight the implications seem obvious, but at the time nothing was clear. Within a week old enemies had become new friends. If Admiral Milne could see no military purpose for *Goeben* in the Aegean, his much more politically conscious superiors in Whitehall were equally blind.

Milne's first thought when he heard the news was to stop her from escaping. The light cruiser *Weymouth* was sent to "blockade" the Dardanelles. Just to see, she called for a pilot and asked for permission to enter as far as Chanak. It was of course denied.

Within the Turkish government there was total disarray. When news was received of the arrival of the German ships, the ambassadors of Russia, France, and Britain pressed the Turks to disarm them. Anxious to preserve her neutrality, Turkey at first agreed. Then the Germans put on pressure. All night the debate wavered to and fro, until a truly Byzantine solution occurred: "Could not the Germans have sold us those ships?"

The solution was masterly. The two warships were being delivered under contract, therefore there was no need to disarm them or intern the crews. Turkish neutrality was not infringed. And besides, it was a wonderful riposte to the British, who had so hastily seized the Turkish battleships *Reshadieh* and *Sultan Osman I* nine days before.

Goeben and *Breslau* were allowed to pass through the Dardanelles to the Sea of Marmara, but the Turkish government was still trying to keep its options open. First the Turks wanted to see which way Bulgaria and Romania would jump; they really would have liked to see which side was going to win the war before committing themselves.

Souchon was installed as Commander-in-Chief of the Turkish Navy, and the British naval mission was expelled. At a ceremony off Constantinople, the German ships were renamed *Sultan Yavuz Selim* and *Midilli*, they ran up the scarlet Turkish flag, and their crews were issued with the fez.

For 12 long weeks Turkey dithered. Churchill proposed going right in after the two ships with a flotilla of torpedo boats to sink them. They might have succeeded, for the Turkish shore defenses were in a deplorable state, but the idea was vetoed on political grounds. The Russians ingenuously proffered a treaty

of friendship, while the French and British ambassadors "alternately blustered and cajolled."[6]

The Germans set about bolstering the defenses of the Dardanelles, refurbishing the tattered Turkish Navy, and securing supplies of coal for their ships. From far across Europe—from Lorraine, the Ardennes, and Flanders; from the forests of East Prussia, over the foothills of Carpathia, and in the valley of the Marne—came the thunder of mighty battles.

Souchon decided to act. On October 27 he set out into the Black Sea at the head of the Turkish fleet, his German Admiral's command flag streaming from the foremast. At dawn on the 29th, ships and shore installations at four ports on the Russian Black Sea coast were subjected to bombardment. No great damage was sustained by the Russians, and the shore batteries at Sevastopol replied with such spirit that they scored two hits on *Sultan Yavuz Selim*, but the ships were close enough to shore to make their identity unmistakable. Every ship flew the scarlet ensign with star and crescent, emblem of the historic enemy of 1854 and 1878.

The Grand Vizier had not been told. Once again Enver, on his own initiative, had allowed the Rear-Admiral to proceed. Turkey ordered the ships to be recalled and talked about offers of apology and compensation. On October 30 the British ambassador called upon Turkey to send home the German crews on board the two ships or to face a state of war.

But the fact was that the battle cruiser swung insolently at her moorings in the Golden Horn, firmly under the control of Souchon and his German crew. The Turkish capital—the national arsenal, the dockyard, the seat of government, and the very palace of the Sultan—lay prostrate under her guns.

Still divided, the Turkish cabinet did nothing. Russia declared war on Turkey on November 2; Britain and France followed suit three days later. Souchon had accomplished his objective.

Plate 32.

EMDEN

Tanahjampea, Dutch East Indies, 1914

The famous light cruiser *Emden* is seen in the Dutch East Indies. Making her way cautiously out of the Pacific and into the Indian Ocean, she avoided passing Singapore and the Strait of Malacca, where she could scarcely have escaped detection and pursuit.

The Netherlands remained neutral in the 1914-18 war in Europe. Sensitive to the fate of neighboring Belgium, whose territory had been violated in the German march against France, Holland was punctilious about observing the rules of neutrality. Warships of the belligerent nations were permitted to stay in her territorial waters for no more than 24 hours in a three-month period.

In the background lies the powerful Dutch coast-defense battleship *Tromp*, armed with two 9.4" and four 6" guns. She was protected by a 6" armored belt. Courtesies were exchanged between the two warships, and Captain Müller of *Emden* was received on board *Tromp* to pay his respects to her commanding officer.

German ships of 1914 exhibited extreme economy in superstructure. Searchlights were carried on platforms on the masts, which were tall in order to elevate the wireless aerials as far as possible.

The spacing of three funnels well forward facilitated disguise. *Emden* successfully masqueraded as a four-funnelled cruiser, which had to be British, by erecting a dummy funnel of wood and canvas astern of her real ones.

CHAPTER VIII

MARCONI AND TELEFUNKEN: THE ANXIOUS SEARCH FOR VON SPEE

If you walk down Whitehall and look up at the copper-green roofs of the Admiralty, you can still see masts and wireless aerials. From these Morse code was stammered out to warships around the world. Relayed first by the big transmitter at Poldhu near the southwest tip of England, signals flashed on from lonely hilltop masts and island stations scattered throughout the distant reaches of the Empire.

In 1914 British seaborne commerce was huge: 19 million tons of shipping. On any one day there would be 3,000 ships at sea. Few of these were equipped with the newfangled Marconi apparatus; if they were attacked they had no means of letting the fact be known.

Wireless telegraphy had played no role before the Russo-Japanese War, but by 1914 it promised to allow naval operations to be directed on a truly global scale. Poring over their charts in the Admiralty War Room, the First Lord, Winston Churchill, and the admirals made their grand dispositions.

As time ran out on August 4, there were ten German warships at large beyond home ports. *Goeben* and *Breslau* formed the Mediterranean Division. The Cruiser Squadron under Vice-Admiral Count Maximilian von Spee was based at Tsingtao, the German treaty port in northern China. It comprised two powerful armored cruisers, *Scharnhorst* and *Gneisenau*, and three light cruisers, *Emden*, *Nürnberg*, and *Leipzig*. The main strength of the squadron was at this moment visiting Ponape in the colony of the Caroline Islands. *Emden* had been left as guardship at Tsingtao, and *Leipzig* was on the west coast of Mexico. Deployed in the Caribbean were *Dresden* and *Karlsruhe*, which had just arrived from home to relieve the former, while *Königsberg*, another light cruiser, had been dispatched to German East Africa. *Dresden*'s last assignment had been to spirit away Huerta, the deposed dictator of Mexico, until he could be of further use to Germany.

The light cruisers were lithe, fast, modern vessels, lightly protected and armed with ten 4.1" guns. The crews of these ships were elite, proud of their skills, and Von Spee's cruisers were the gunnery champions of the German navy.

German warships were supported by a worldwide clandestine supply and intelligence organization. With naval needs in mind, the country's merchantmen had been supplied with Telefunken wireless equipment. In the event of war, they were to make themselves available as supply ships or for conversion to armed raiders.

Against the threat of commerce raiders, the Royal Navy had disposed around the world roughly 30 cruisers, a mixture of obsolete and modern, 12 of which were armored ships. Australia had a battle cruiser and two light cruisers, and the French and Russian navies east of Suez each comprised two units. Within ten days Japan entered the war, and a whole new navy was added to the Allied forces in the Pacific, but no Dreadnoughts could be spared from the Grand Fleet without endangering its narrow superiority in the North Sea.

The temptation to run things from London was irresistible, but intervention from such a distance

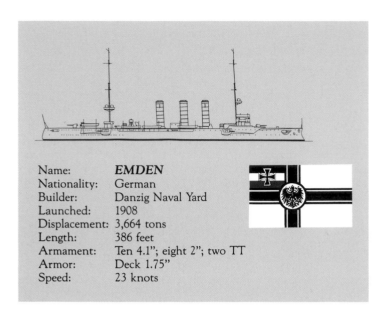

Name: **EMDEN**
Nationality: German
Builder: Danzig Naval Yard
Launched: 1908
Displacement: 3,664 tons
Length: 386 feet
Armament: Ten 4.1"; eight 2"; two TT
Armor: Deck 1.75"
Speed: 23 knots

was by no means always helpful. Radio reception was erratic; interpretation, unreliable. Coded transmissions put out by Telefunken apparatus could be distinguished from Marconi, but the science of radio direction finding had still to be developed. The range of an intercepted transmission might be roughly gauged from its strength, but a ship's vision was limited to the horizon at a distance of no more than about 12 miles, with a little more added for funnel smoke.

Von Spee's cruisers simply vanished into the enormous wastes of the Pacific. For weeks and weeks they escaped detection. Once one of the German cruisers put in to Honolulu for supplies. Another time some of von Spee's ships appeared disconcertingly at Tahiti to shell the French shore installations. There was speculation in London as to whether the Germans would be allowed to transit the newly opened Panama Canal, but Britain's main anxiety was that von Spee would double back and fall upon troop convoys leaving Australia for Europe.

Finally a faintly heard transmission was intercepted, suggesting that the Vice-Admiral was heading for Easter Island. Not until late October was the squadron, reinforced now by *Leipzig* and *Dresden*, positively reported off the coast of Chile.

For all the attempt to direct events with Olympian reach from Whitehall, an inferior British force was there to meet von Spee. Rear-Admiral Sir Christopher Cradock had under his command two big armored cruisers, manned by reservists; a fast modern light cruiser; and an armed merchantman. The elderly battleship that had also been assigned to his command, *Canopus*, was unable to keep up for lack of speed. His armored cruisers *Good Hope* and *Monmouth* were outclassed by the Germans; not only were they slower, they were armed mainly with 6" guns, which were outranged by the *Scharnhorst* and *Gneisenau*, and half of these were mounted in lower casemates that were so close to the waterline as to be useless in a heavy sea.

Cradock was impetuous. Mindful of the scorn that had been heaped on his contemporary Troubridge, Cradock had no hesitation in tackling a superior enemy. Once von Spee was found, he must be given no chance to escape.

The British light cruiser *Glasgow* had been sent on ahead to the Chilean port of Coronel, where she picked up wireless transmissions indicating the presence of German ships. In a rising sea the British ships headed straight for the expected position of the enemy.

Von Spee, steaming southwest, encountered Cradock's squadron 50 miles off the coast at dusk. With his superior speed he was able to keep the British ships at extreme range as the sun sank over the angry waters behind them. At the instant of sunset, the German ships became lost to view against the dark mass of the coastline, while the British were silhouetted against the afterglow.

Cautiously von Spee closed the range. *Good*

Hope's forward 9.2" gun was disabled within minutes, leaving a single gun on the British side with sufficient range to reach the enemy. The expert gunners on the German cruisers steadily reduced their targets to a shambles.

Glasgow, matched against *Leipzig* with her lighter armament of 4.1" guns, remained relatively untouched. She escaped after the battle, and from her crew came the harrowing description of the end of *Good Hope*. An hour after sunset the flagship was shaken by a violent explosion, and shortly afterwards the sinister glow of internal fires was extinguished as she was swamped by the sea.

Monmouth, though fearfully battered, managed to break away from the enemy in the darkness and to put out her raging fires. She was desperately unlucky to be encountered by *Nürnberg*, hurrying to rejoin the rest of von Spee's squadron. The British cruiser refused demands to surrender, although she was listing so heavily that none of her guns could be brought to bear, and *Nürnberg* had no difficulty in sinking her. There were no survivors from either *Monmouth* or *Good Hope*.

Whitehall was appalled. Admiral Lord Fisher had just been recalled as First Sea Lord. Commands were given. The Grand Fleet, after all, could manage without three battle cruisers for a few weeks.

Secretly and swiftly, *Invincible* and *Inflexible* were withdrawn from the Cromarty Firth, replenished at Devonport, and dispatched to the South Atlantic under the command of Vice-Admiral Sir Doveton Sturdee.

A third battle cruiser, *Princess Royal*, was sent to the West Indies in case von Spee should attempt the Panama Canal, and Australian and Japanese squadrons were directed to converge towards the west coast of South America. The forces of retribution were being gathered.

Meanwhile von Spee was in a somber mood. Appreciating how slender were the chances of his squadron getting home, he refused to be drawn into celebrations at Valparaiso. He led his ships out to sea and then covertly south to the fjord-like Gulf of Peñas. Arrangements were made for coal supplies to meet his ships at Pernambuco and New York.

On December 2 the German squadron rounded the Horn. The weather at the Cape of Storms lived up to its evil reputation, and the ships became separated in tempestuous seas. The light cruisers were even obliged to throw overboard the coal that had been loaded on deck.

The German consulate in Valparaiso, apprised of the dispatch of British battle cruisers, tried vainly to contact the flagship, but she was cut off from wireless communication by the bleak mountains of Tierra del Fuego.

The day after this stormy passage, *Leipzig* encountered a British four-masted barque flying the red ensign. She proved to be *Drummuir*, laden with 2,800 tons of good Welsh steam coal, no doubt intended for Cradock. Taking her under tow, *Leipzig* headed for the sheltered waters of the Beagle Channel, where the other ships of the German squadron gathered to take on their share of this windfall. For three days they lay in the wild and splendid setting while coaling took place, and von Spee conferred with his captains. He determined, against advice, to make a raid on the British base in the Falklands in order to destroy the wireless station and rattle the enemy before making his way north.

Sturdee, completely in the dark as to von Spee's whereabouts, was at the same time steaming leisurely southward. The old cruiser *Vindictive*, then a wireless experimental ship with exaggeratedly tall topmasts, was detached in mid-Atlantic to act as a signal relay station. He met the five British cruisers of the South America Station off the coast of Brazil and finally reached Port Stanley in the Falklands on December 7, barely one day before his adversary.

In the inner harbor at Stanley was the old battle-

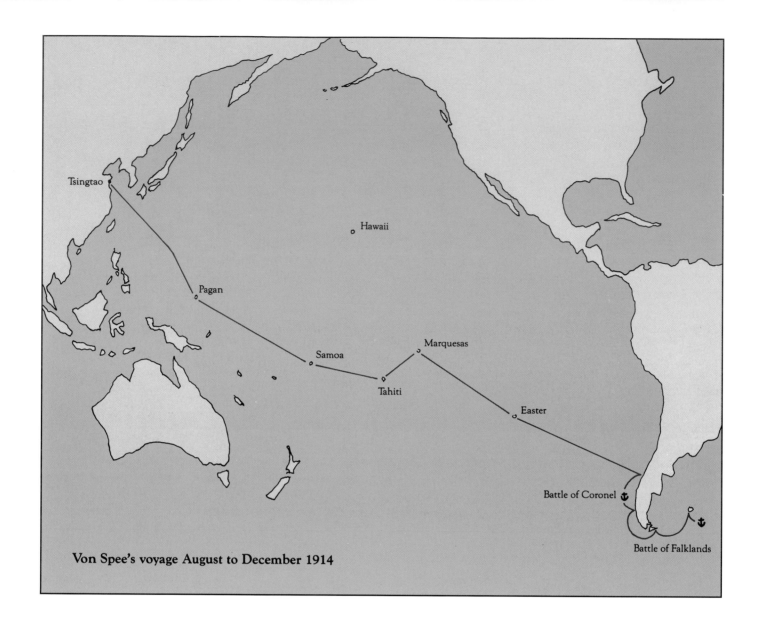

Von Spee's voyage August to December 1914

ship *Canopus*. Too slow to keep up with Cradock's cruisers, she had been sent back through the Strait of Magellan and ordered to take up station for harbor defense. She was carefully sited behind low-lying land, settled onto the mud, and observation posts were set up on shore connected by landline. On the morning of December 8 she was due to demonstrate her gunnery to the Commander-in-Chief, and late the night before the crew of one turret, to steal a march on the other, stealthily loaded their guns with practice rounds.

Soon after dawn of the long summer's day, von Spee's scouting force, *Gneisenau* and *Nürnberg*, was spotting approaching from the south. Sturdee was caught napping, his flagship in the act of coaling, and only one British ship was on less than two hours' notice for steam. *Canopus* even had difficulty in alerting Sturdee to the news; a gun had to be fired and a searchlight trained on *Invincible*'s bridge, so engrossed was she in coaling and enveloped in clouds of dust.

Gneisenau was in for no less of a surprise. First

she saw in the clear sky a tall column of smoke, which she took to be coal stocks being burned. Next she made out a thicket of masts and funnels. Finally, with sickening apprehension, she made out the characteristic tripod masts, two pairs, which could only mean the presence of capital ships.

At that moment *Canopus* achieved her moment of glory. Opening fire from concealment with her 12" guns, she scored a hit with her second salvo. No one on *Gneisenau* could know that the ricochet was only a practice round, so her captain decided to beat a hasty retreat.

Sturdee was lucky. A determined attack at that moment would have been damaging, and it might well have resulted in a ship sunk in the fairway, for another half an hour passed before the British battle cruisers were able to get under way.

Thereafter events unfolded in a predictable way. The battle cruisers gave chase. With an advantage of 3 or 4 knots in speed, they steadily overhauled the German armored cruisers, and though a following wind caused them to be hampered by dense funnel smoke, their far heavier armament of 12" guns began to have its inevitable effect. Proof against the Germans' 8.2" shells at anything greater than 10,000 yards, *Invincible* and *Inflexible* had only to maintain their range in order to hammer the enemy with impunity. The tables had been turned.

Von Spee gallantly ordered his light cruisers to escape, fearlessly turning towards the enemy with his two heavier units. Sturdee, anxious to avoid damage to the precious battle cruisers, veered away and kept his distance. The German ships were hard pressed, and when they turned away for relief, the British battle cruisers plunged through the cloud of smoke, emerging on the enemy's quarter. At last the British ships could clearly see their targets and mark the fall of shot. Von Spee fought back valiantly, twice more turning in vain attempts to close the range, but one after the other his armored cruisers

were overwhelmed by the heavier weight of gunfire. Fires raged beyond control, and each eventually capsized in the icy Antarctic water. During the final agony a stately tall ship glided under full sail between the embattled lines of warships. Gunlayers glued to their eyepieces experienced a frisson: who could say if she were real?

The three German light cruisers detached at an early stage in the battle were chased by Sturdee's cruisers. Two were caught and sunk, but *Dresden* outran her pursuers. She eluded them for a further three months before being eventually run to earth in the Juan Fernández Islands.

Protagonists of the battle cruiser were delighted, most of all Lord Fisher. The Battle of the Falklands had handsomely vindicated his faith in the new type as a counter to the most powerful of armored raiders.

The hunt for von Spee, however, held another significance that was less immediately evident. The science of wireless telegraphy had made its first serious impact on naval strategy.

Signaling range suddenly leapt far beyond the visible horizon. Marconi and Telefunken apparatus foreshadowed the techniques of radio direction finding, radar, asdic, and the whole array of electronic surveillance, computing, and guidance systems, which are now the most critical elements of a warship's capacity.

Two of von Spee's light cruisers had been detached on missions of their own. After the outbreak of war, *Emden* sailed from Tsingtao to join the Squadron in the Mariana Islands, but at her captain's request she alone turned back to the west to raid British commerce in the Indian Ocean. *Königsberg* was already in East Africa; her story will come later.

Emden's voyage became something of a legend. Captain von Müller was bold and resourceful, and by his chivalrous behavior he earned universal respect. The little cruiser was able to elude pursuit for two months, causing untold disruption. She

Plate 33.

KÖNIGSBERG

Pangani River Mouth, German East Africa, 1913

The light cruiser *Königsberg* enters the mouth of the Pangani River. She was one of eight German cruisers overseas at the outbreak of war to receive orders to become commerce raiders. Owing to engine defects *Königsberg*'s raiding career was short-lived, and she was obliged to conceal herself in the delta of the Rufigi River. There she was tracked down and sunk by the Royal Navy.

Pangani is one of many Arab settlements on the East African coast that was captured by the Portuguese in the seventeenth century.

Forts were set up at many points around Africa in order to secure the trade route to India and the Far East. At each place Casuarina trees were planted. Their fronds, floating far out to sea, would guide Portuguese ships toward a safe anchorage along a coastline that was mostly barred by coral reefs.

The flag hoist V over J indicates, in international code, "I require assistance, am going to signal by semaphore." Naval Code would not have been used to address the Customs House on the waterfront.

captured 22 prizes and sank two warships before finally being cornered and brought to bay.

To find a ship in the open sea was no easy task before the days of aircraft or radar. Outside the principal shipping lanes, a ship could pass unseen for weeks. In the course of a 12-hour day, a searching cruiser might scan about 5,000 square miles; the Indian Ocean encompasses 28 million. Since *Emden*'s purpose was to raid commerce, it became a matter of wits to predict where and when she might appear. Without wireless, her victims were unable to call for help, and days might pass before naval authorities learned of an attack.

Emden's overriding problem was coal. She had at her disposal a German collier, and she took coal from many of her prizes, but the constant nagging concern for replenishing her bunkers was never absent. The physical job of coaling was always slow, tough, and filthy labor, but for *Emden* the need to perform it at sea made the operation doubly onerous. To do so required a sheltered spot, and there was always the worry about being caught in the middle of the process.

Early in September *Emden* emerged through the neutral islands of the Dutch East Indies and entered the Bay of Bengal. She made for the regular steamer route off the east coast of India, where she fell upon freighters like a fox among chickens. Within a few days she had taken on board so many men from sunken vessels that she stopped a neutral ship to transfer them. The Italian captain refused, turned back toward Calcutta, and reported his encounter to the liner he met emerging from the mouth of the Hooghly. The latter was equipped with Marconi, and the first word of the raider was broadcast to the world.

Royal Navy forces in the region were not extensive. The admiral of the China Station had two armored cruisers and two light cruisers at his disposal; *Hampshire* alone was in the Indian Ocean.

Signals flashed out, and British, French, and Jap-

anese ships converged. Müller wisely left the area. Much of his success was due to intelligent listening; he rarely used his own transmitter, but he was able to guess much from the traffic he overheard.

Müller's next move involved a dashing attack on Madras. The city was lit up as in peacetime, including all coastal navigation lights, when *Emden* approached on the evening of September 22, 1914. A few salvos set on fire the oil storage depot. Militarily the lightning raid was of no great consequence, but psychologically, its impact was huge. Britain had controlled things for so many years in this part of the world that foreign intervention was unthinkable, and the whole panoply of British control depended ultimately on prestige.

Müller melted away again, this time passing south of Ceylon and finding six more victims off the west coast of India. By the time the one ship that was not sunk reached Colombo, *Emden* was hundreds of miles to the south. Newspapers on board the captured vessels gave the Germans useful intelligence of intended shipping movements.

The spot chosen by Müller for rest and recuperation was the tiny island of Diego Garcia in the middle of the Indian Ocean. Today it is leased to the United

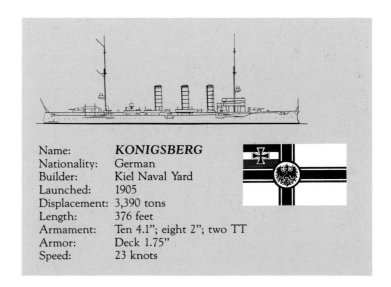

Name:	**KONIGSBERG**
Nationality:	German
Builder:	Kiel Naval Yard
Launched:	1905
Displacement:	3,390 tons
Length:	376 feet
Armament:	Ten 4.1"; eight 2"; two TT
Armor:	Deck 1.75"
Speed:	23 knots

States as a military base, but in September 1914 it was so infrequented that the British manager of the coconut plantation was unaware of the outbreak of war. Consequently, the Germans were extended every courtesy.

By this time the Admiralty in London was becoming extremely irritated, while in the Indian Ocean the hue and cry was growing. Cruisers were sent to the Maldives and on the routes leading back toward Sumatra; colliers waiting there for *Emden* had been discovered and detained. Wireless traffic indicated that shipping had been resumed westward from Ceylon, so Müller returned to his hunting ground off the Malabar Coast, narrowly missing *Hampshire* on the way. Seven more prizes were taken.

Emden slipped away again in squally weather, heading eastward while the pursuit galloped west. A month after the raid on Madras, she cruised quietly before dawn into the busy roadstead of Penang, on the west coast of Malaya. Disguised with a false extra funnel and flying British colors, she was not molested as she slipped into the channel between George Town and the mainland. Lying close to shore was *Zemchug*, a ten-year-old Russian cruiser, veteran of the Battle of Tsushima.

Emden launched a torpedo at the sleeping cruiser, turned tightly amongst the shipping, fired a second, and swiftly withdrew. *Zemchug* was hit by both missiles, the second of which caused a large explosion and sank the ship before her crew managed to reach action stations.

On her way out to sea, *Emden* encountered a merchantman, whom she stopped, but on the approach of a small French destroyer, the boarding party was recalled. In a brief action the French warship was sunk by the cruiser's overwhelmingly superior gunfire.

After Penang Müller decided to make a rendezvous with one of his supply ships near Direction Island in the Cocos (Keeling) group, south of Sumatra.

This was the site of an important cable and wireless relay station.

The Admiralty at this stage was focusing on the safety of a troop convoy of 36 ships carrying 30,000 men that was about to sail from Australia to Europe. Four warships were assigned to its escort: two Australian light cruisers, the armored cruiser *Minotaur*, and the Japanese battle cruiser *Ibuki*.

Müller made his first mistake. As he approached Direction Island, he saw that the lagoon offered a sheltered anchorage for coaling, so he summoned his collier by wireless. For once someone ashore was thoroughly alert. The island operator recognized the transmission as suspicious, challenged, and as *Emden* approached the harbor entrance, the news went out over the air, as well as by undersea cable.

Emden's men were, as always, punctilious and correct. The landing party destroyed the cable and wireless installations, but they did no harm to civilian personnel.

Interestingly, *Minotaur* had been detached from the convoy escort and was headed for South Africa, where an ugly situation had arisen. Receiving the signal from Direction Island, she called back the island operator, but by now the mast was down, and she received no reply. *Emden*, listening as usual, heard the transmission and correctly placed it several hundred miles to the west. Little did the cruiser's radio man know that a convoy and its powerful escort were at that moment passing within two hours' steaming distance.

The convoy commander dispatched the Australian cruiser *Sydney* to deal with *Emden*. It was enough.

Sydney arrived just as the German landing party was getting ready to leave. *Emden* did not wait. She weighed anchor and swung out to sea to meet her opponent, working up to full speed. Her 4.1" guns were no match for *Sydney*'s battery of 6" guns, and her shells were unable to penetrate the other ship's 2" armored belt. Although *Emden* fought with great

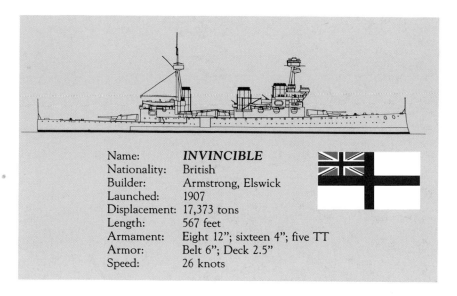

Name:	**INVINCIBLE**
Nationality:	British
Builder:	Armstrong, Elswick
Launched:	1907
Displacement:	17,373 tons
Length:	567 feet
Armament:	Eight 12"; sixteen 4"; five TT
Armor:	Belt 6"; Deck 2.5"
Speed:	26 knots

gallantry, the contest was not prolonged; almost completely wrecked, she was eventually run ashore on the coral reef of Cocos Island.

Captain Müller and the surviving crew members were only rescued with great difficulty because of the heavy surf. Thus, the landing party that had been abandoned on Direction Island had time to get away. Fifty sailors under the cruiser's First Officer commandeered the wireless company's schooner and managed to sail to Java. There they took over a German tug in which they made their way to the Red Sea. After an extraordinary series of adventures amongst Arabs, some hostile and some friendly, they made contact with Turkish forces who got them to Constantinople. A hero's welcome awaited them at home.

For the story of the last of von Spee's cruisers, it is necessary to return to 1903. In that year a book was published in England entitled "The Riddle of the Sands," by Erskine Childers. A splendid, elegantly written spy story, it was created for a political purpose.

In the early years of the century, the author, who was a reserve naval officer, became convinced of the seriousness of German ambitions and of the threat to the east coast of England. Ignored by the authorities, he determined to awake public opinion by means of a novel. His book was widely read, and his ideas were taken seriously in many quarters.

One outcome was that the Admiralty, on the outbreak of war with Germany in 1914, commandeered three river gunboats then under construction by Vickers for Brazil. Classified as monitors, these vessels mounted two 6" guns on a hull with 50' beam but only 4'6" draft. Unlike their famous American prototype, they were not armored ships.

The Admiralty intended to employ the craft in the neighborhood of The Wash, which Childers had identified in his novel as the destination for German landing craft. Other British warships were unable to enter such shallow waters.

The monitors *Severn* and *Mersey* carried out patrol duties on the east coast of England during the opening months of the war, but they were then called upon to undertake a very different kind of operation.

One of the great rivers of East Africa, the Rufiji, emerges into the Indian Ocean 100 miles south of Dar-es-Salaam, capital of what was at that time German East Africa. The mouth of the river forms a delta, a great confusing maze of channels and mangrove swamps. Twelve miles in from the open sea in one of the shallow tidal creeks lie the remains of the German cruiser *Königsberg*.

Not a great deal remains to be seen today. The rusted port side of the main deck shows above swirling brown water at low tide, but the masts, funnels, and upperworks have long since collapsed and disintegrated into the mud.

At the time of her completion in 1912, the slim, elegant cruiser capable of 24 knots was the showpiece of the Imperial Navy. She was assigned to escort the Kaiser's yacht on his visit to Cowes Week, and in April 1914 she was sent to represent the Navy at the forthcoming Great African Exposition in Dar-es-Salaam.

Plate 34.

INVINCIBLE and INFLEXIBLE

Battle of the Falklands, 1914

The two British battle cruisers *Invincible* and *Inflexible* opened fire with their heavy guns on von Spee's armored cruisers at the Battle of the Falklands on December 8, 1914. They had been dispatched to the South Atlantic to recover the situation after the disaster of Coronel, and they carried out their mission conclusively and without serious damage. It was a textbook demonstration of their capability.

Invincible was the original of all battle cruisers. The type was designed in response to the large Russian and French armored cruisers built from 1895 to 1905. Von Spee's big cruisers *Scharnhorst* and *Gneisenau* were more menacing commerce raiders, with 14 medium-caliber guns and a top speed of 23 knots, but *Invincible* was twice their size. Her 12" guns outranged the German 8.2" guns, and she had a margin of 3 knots in speed.

The British ships are flying several battle ensigns, a precaution in case a flag was shot away in action. Eighteen months after the Falklands, *Invincible* herself was sunk at the Battle of Jutland.

This celebration was to mark the completion of the railway to Kigoma, on Lake Tanganyika, nearly 800 miles inland, and the Kaiser himself was due to attend the ceremonies in August.

Events in Europe intervened. *Königsberg*, like the other cruisers, had orders to engage in commerce raiding in the event of war. Warned of its imminence, she quit Dar-es-Salaam and effortlessly evaded the slower British cruisers, which had been detailed to keep an eye on her. There were three of these off the coast of East Africa; the elderly *Hyacinth*, *Pegasus*, and *Astraea*.

Königsberg steamed first for a point near Aden where shipping routes converge towards the mouth of the Red Sea. She quickly intercepted a merchantman named *City of Winchester*, which became the first British ship to be captured during the war. Acting in concert with a German merchant ship, to whom she transferred the crew of the captured vessel, *Königsberg* replenished her bunkers before sinking her prize. She then moved south and stationed herself for three weeks in the vicinity of the north end of Madagascar, but without success. Now in further need of coal, she made a rendezvous with a German collier at the mouth of the river Rufiji.

Her next exploit was a night raid on the roadstead at Zanzibar, where she had learned that the cruiser *Pegasus* was lying complacently while her boilers were being repaired. It took only minutes for the well-trained gunlayers of *Königsberg* to dispose of their target, but in the ship's hurry to leave the scene, she failed to destroy the cable station. Ironically, as *Königsberg* withdrew she herself became the victim of an engine defect.

The obvious place to head for would have been Dar-es-Salaam, but the harbor mouth there had been blocked by the Germans themselves, who had sunk a floating dock in the channel to forestall a British attack. *Königsberg* therefore returned to the mouth of the Rufiji, concealing herself in one of the many shallow branches of the delta.

The Rufiji Delta, one of the most unhealthy places in the world, is atrociously hot and humid. The air is thick with insects, and the muddy water seethes with leeches and unpleasant reptiles. In 1914 malaria, bilharzia, yellow fever, and sleeping sickness were serious hazards.

The landward approach is very difficult, a Tarzan-like jungle of tangled growth with great reaches of tidal swamp. The climate is stifling, and every afternoon the clouds build up until they finally unburden themselves in a mighty deluge, accompanied by symphonies of thunder.

For the British, injured pride was followed by a ponderous mustering of resources. The search for *Königsberg* extended to Madagascar and along the coastline of Africa as far as 1,700 miles to the south. Three fast modern cruisers mounting 6" guns were devoted to the task.

For the Germans, the mechanical problem proved to be a fractured engine block, which required the services of a foundry for repair. Any kind of strenuous exertion in that climate requires tremendous determination. Hundreds of Africans were employed to clear a path through thick bush, and by an amazing feat the heavy component was dragged on sledges for more than 100 miles to Dar-es-Salaam.

The British search went on for five anxious weeks. It was helped by a bold cutting-out expedition in small boats that found evidence aboard a German merchantman in the harbor at Lindi and by information gleaned from local Africans along the coast.

Eventually the cruiser *Chatham* spotted the masts of *Königsberg*, just visible above the crests of mangrove trees. The enemy was located nine miles from the open sea, well beyond the range of the cruiser's 6" guns.

The British faced a major difficulty. The eight mouths of the Rufiji are separated by a maze of islands and floating vegetation. A coral reef extends six miles off shore, and in the channels there is a sandbar, which is covered by no more than five feet of water at low tide. Spring tides rise as much as 15 feet. The draft of the cruisers, British and German, was about 18 feet.

Since the British lacked detailed hydrographic surveys, the course and depth of channels was largely unknown. A colorful character called Pretorius was enlisted to help. An Afrikaaner hunter, he had made his home in the Rufiji Delta, but he had fallen afoul of the Germans before the war. He volunteered to be put ashore to explore the waterways, where his local experience enabled him to evade detection, and he took soundings from an open boat.

The first attempt to sink *Königsberg* involved trying to approach from the sea close enough to shell her. *Chatham*'s guns had a range of seven and a half miles, but with the risk of stranding on coral or mudbank, she was unable to get quite close enough, and the German cruiser withdrew progressively further and further upriver into the jungle.

Fire-control stations were established by the Germans on islands and on adjoining higher ground, and some of the cruiser's smaller guns were mounted, together with torpedoes, field guns and Maxims, in concealed entrenchments near the river mouths.

Accompanied by a flotilla of smaller craft, the British tried to enter the river by steam picketboat armed with torpedoes. This attack was frustrated by the German defenses, and *Königsberg* was eased and warped yet further up the Rufiji.

For their next attempt the British sank a blockship in the principal channel. It was a hazardous operation, many casualties were incurred, and the outcome was inconclusive. The blockship, it was considered, might not have completely closed the channel, and there

Plate 35.

QUEEN ELIZABETH

Forth Bridge, Scotland, 1915

The new battleship passes majestically beneath the Forth Bridge in 1915, with the fortified island of Inchgarvie beyond her and the Dalmeny shore in the background. The impressive cantilever bridge is of tubular steel construction, some members being as much as 12 feet in diameter.

The five *Queen Elizabeth*-class fast battleships that joined the Grand Fleet in 1915 and early 1916 were equipped with the new 15"-caliber gun, and they were the first to use exclusively oil-fired boilers. *Queen Elizabeth*

herself took part in the Gallipoli campaign, trying to reduce the forts in the Dardanelles by firing blind over the intervening peninsula. She was not present at Jutland, but Admiral Beatty hoisted his flag on her when he succeeded Jellicoe as Commander-in-Chief in the last two years of the war. Thus she was flagship of the triumphant armada that sailed to meet the surrendered German High Seas Fleet off the Firth of Forth on November 21, 1918.

These handsome battleships finally achieved

an apt balance of firepower, speed, and protection, which made them the most effective fighting ships of their era. All five of them survived to render service in the Second World War.

remained some doubt as to whether *Königsberg* could not, perhaps, slip out by one of the other mouths.

Next to be tried was the use of airplanes. A Curtiss seaplane was shipped from Durban on board a Union Castle liner. The high temperature and humidity made it difficult for the early type of aircraft to get airborne or to gain altitude. Even today, the daily buildup of thunderheads and the turbulence make this a difficult area for flying. Nevertheless the primitive airplane did succeed in confirming the *Königsberg*'s latest position of refuge.

The first plane crashed and another was lost after engine failure during a reconnaissance over the delta. Two Sopwith seaplanes sent out from England proved scarcely more reliable, and they were incapable of rising off the water while loaded with bombs.

A scheme was hatched to send a silenced motor launch upriver by night to fire a torpedo, but this proposal was vetoed.

It had occurred to someone in London that the two shallow-draft monitors, which were no longer necessary for patrolling The Wash, would be well suited to navigating the shoals of the Rufiji. Had they not been designed for the Amazon?

Severn and *Mersey* were dispatched on the long, weary passage under tow all the way around the coast of Western Europe, through the length of the Mediterranean, via the Suez Canal and the Red Sea, and finally down the steamy coast of Africa as far as Zanzibar.

Four new airplanes were also shipped to the scene:

two Caudrons and two Henry Farmans. They were brought ashore and assembled at a makeshift airstrip on the captured island of Mafia. These landplanes had a slightly better performance than seaplanes; at least they could get two men into the air, but they rarely managed to get their crews safely back again without some element of drama.

The final assault on *Königsberg* made by the two monitors was a tricky business, for *Königsberg*'s broadside of five 4.1" guns was by no means outranged by the less modern 6" weapons of *Severn* and *Mersey*. The monitors grounded more than once, and they encountered great difficulty with the strong tidal currents. Under fire from the shore defenses, they made their way some five miles up the channel, whereupon well directed salvos from the cruiser nearly swamped them.

The monitors were firing blind across intervening islands at more than a five-mile range. A vital element in the action was the corrections to the fall of shot provided by observers in the shaky airplanes. Thus aircraft made their first contribution to naval warfare.

While *Mersey* was badly damaged in the first engagement, on the second day both monitors' guns managed to find the range. A shell penetrated to *Königsberg*'s magazine, the cruiser was torn by a major explosion, and her wreck settled onto the mud so close beneath the keel.

The last of von Spee's elusive raiders had finally been dispatched, eleven months after the outbreak of war.

Name:	**QUEEN ELIZABETH**
Nationality:	British
Builder:	Portsmouth Dockyard
Launched:	1913
Displacement:	27,500 tons
Length:	646 feet
Armament:	Eight 15"; sixteen 6"; two 3"; four TT
Armor:	Belt 13"; Deck 3"
Speed:	23 knots

CHAPTER IX

THE QUEEN ELIZABETH CLASS

A new class of battleships was laid down by Britain in the year 1912. Once in a while a combination of qualities gives rise to a design that is just right, consummately matched to the requirements it is called upon to meet. Such a case was that of the *Queen Elizabeth* class, the last ships to be designed under the aegis of Sir Philip Watts.

Just as Jackie Fisher's drive and enthusiasm was the real thrust behind the creation of *Dreadnought*, the man behind the *Queen Elizabeths* was the new First Lord of the Admiralty, Winston Churchill. It was he who put his weight behind the decision to rush forward production of the proposed new 15" gun.

The standard heavy gun among pre-Dreadnought battleships had been of 12" caliber, and this size was adopted for the all-big-gun ships. In 1910 Britain raised the stakes, as it were, by bringing in the 13.5" gun. The heavier the gun, the larger the shell and the thicker the armor needed to resist it. Germany retained 11" caliber until the *König* class mounted 12" in 1914. Both navies were well aware that German ships carried more armor; they had to, to be on equal terms, for they had larger shells to resist, but the deliberate emphasis by Britain on speed and weight of firepower carried an implicit element of risk. The design of the ships embodied the offensive spirit of the service: the navy's job was to catch the enemy's ships and to sink them.

To understand the implications of the increased caliber of gun, it is necessary to digress a little into the realm of ballistics. The weight and therefore the penetrating and explosive power of a 15" shell was roughly three times that of an 11" one. Moreover, the trajectory of a projectile is affected by aerodynamic drag, and while the mass of a shell varies as the cube of its caliber, the drag varies only as its square, so at a given muzzle velocity, the larger shell carries further than the smaller one.

There had recently been a drastic reappraisal of the likely ranges at which battles would be fought. In the 1890s target practice had taken place at a mile (1,760 yards), but by 1900 this had increased to 6,000 yards, the range at which fire was opened at Tsushima. By 1908 the doctrine was that 10,000 yards, which was just about the normal limit of visibility in the North Sea, was the likely battle range. Armor protection was designed with this sort of range in mind. Shells of 12" caliber, for example, would be descending at an angle of nine degrees on impact at this range.

As range is increased the effect of drag becomes more pronounced, as it does on a shuttlecock in a game of Badminton. To achieve greater range the gun is elevated more steeply, but the angle of descent becomes steeper still. Muzzle velocity plays a diminishing role.

At the Battle of Jutland the battle cruiser action was fought at 15,000 to 20,000 yards. At the greater range 11" shells were plunging at steeper than 45 degrees when they hit. The destruction of British battle cruisers arose, in the first place, as a result of this fact. The action was fought at far greater range than designers had considered possible in 1906, and

Plate 36.

ROYAL OAK

Battle of Jutland, 1916

Turning hard to port at more than 20 knots, the new battleship *Royal Oak* follows the flagship *Iron Duke* as she swings away to avoid torpedoes launched by enemy destroyers at 7:22 p.m. In the gathering dusk the German High Seas Fleet had just blundered for the second time into the long, deadly line of Jellicoe's battleships.

Reports describe the patchy visibility, further obscured by cordite and funnel smoke, and the confused sea caused by so many ships and shells churning up the shallow waters off the Danish coast. Ships were dwarfed by fountains thrown up by heavy-caliber shellfire.

Royal Oak was sunk on October 14, 1939, by the German submarine U47, which had daringly penetrated the net defenses of Scapa Flow and scored hits with three torpedoes. Her four sister ships of the *Royal Sovereign* class served throughout the Second World War. *Royal Sovereign* herself was transferred for five years to the Soviet navy as part of the Lend-Lease operation. Some thought that they detected irony in the choice of this particular ship to send to Stalin.

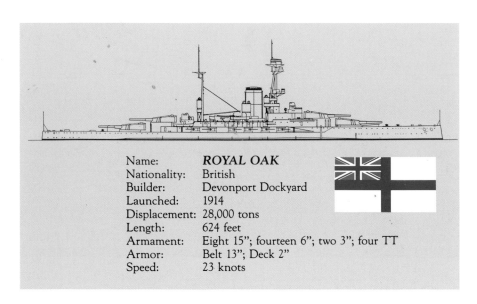

Name: **ROYAL OAK**
Nationality: British
Builder: Devonport Dockyard
Launched: 1914
Displacement: 28,000 tons
Length: 624 feet
Armament: Eight 15"; fourteen 6"; two 3"; four TT
Armor: Belt 13"; Deck 2"
Speed: 23 knots

shells penetrated decks and turret roofs rather than meeting the armored belt. Larger shells, used by British ships, had a flatter trajectory than the German 11" projectiles.

Queen Elizabeth's 15" caliber guns had a range of 24,000 yards, the extreme limit of visibility from a spotting top. (In the 1930s their range was increased to 37,000 yards or 20 miles.) The muzzle velocity of the 15" guns was lower than that of the 12" and 13.5" models; this meant less wear and thus longer barrel life, and it also gave the guns more consistency or a smaller spread between successive rounds.

The seemingly small increase in the diameter of the bore of Queen Elizabeth's guns conferred an additional weight of shell and penetrating power and an increase in effective range far out of proportion to the increment in size.

The main guns in Queen Elizabeth were disposed in four twin turrets superimposed fore and aft to obtain the maximum all-round field of fire. The layout had been pioneered by South Carolina, completed in 1910, and it became classic. Bismarck in 1940 and the last battleship ever built, Vanguard in 1946, found no better layout for their heavy guns.

Trials in Thunderer in 1912 had demonstrated finally and conclusively that centralized fire control activated electrically was more effective than shooting by individual guns. The inevitable refinement was a computerized input to anticipate the projected relative positions of two moving ships. By 1913 Dreyer fire-control tables were being installed in all British battleships, but they were dependent on the quality of information supplied by range finders of the day. Range finders had found their way into the Royal Navy in 1892, and by 1912 battleships were equipped with 9-foot instruments. Power and range derived largely from size, and the Queen Elizabeths went one step further by mounting 15-foot models, one on every turret to back up the principal range finder, which was in an armored hood on top of the conning tower. They were the first ships to be built with an entire fire-control system complete from inception.

The adoption of the 15" gun enabled the new ships to deliver a greater weight of broadside than preceding classes with only eight guns in place of ten. By accepting a reduced number of guns, additional space and displacement could be devoted to boilers and power plant. It was decided to take the opportunity to create a division of fast battleships, not just a little faster but almost the equal of battle cruisers in speed, which would be capable of turning the head of the enemy's battle line as Togo had done at Tsushima.

The decision to go for a big advance in speed brought with it the change to oil fuel. It was a risky move. Coal, mined in the British Isles, was the very

foundation of British heavy industry; the best steam coal in the world came from the seams of South Wales. Oil supplies might depend on the fortunes of some despotic regime in Mexico. Oil needed tankers to ship it home and a whole new infrastructure on shore as well as at sea.

But the advantages were compelling. Forty per-cent less weight was needed for the same endurance. Higher boiler pressures were possible, conferring greater speeds. Refueling ship was faster, and boiler room crews could be reduced. Finally, oil possessed the substantial if less tangible benefit of doing away forever with the horrors of coaling.

Within the ship, the absence of coal as a means of

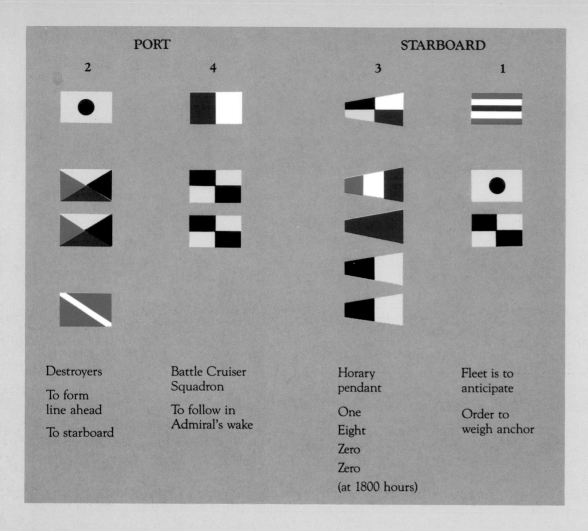

PORT		STARBOARD	
2	**4**	**3**	**1**

Destroyers	Battle Cruiser Squadron	Horary pendant	Fleet is to anticipate
To form line ahead	To follow in Admiral's wake	One	Order to weigh anchor
To starboard		Eight	
		Zero	
		Zero	
		(at 1800 hours)	

Plate 37.

LION

Cromarty Firth, May 1916

Toward the end of May, the hills on both sides of the Cromarty Firth are afire with the yellow bloom of whin and broom. In the background lie the hills of Morangie Forest in Easter Ross, with the whitewashed houses of the village of Invergordon on the shore.

Vice-Admiral David Beatty's flagship *Lion* is lying nearer to the Black Isle, on the south side of the Firth.

Properly, the White Ensign should be worn at the stern and the Union flag at the jack staff on the bow while at anchor. In wartime, however, the ensign was often flown from the mainmast gaff, as at sea. The Vice-Admiral's flag is at the foremast peak. *Lion* is flying four hoists of signal flags, which are illustrated above.

On the left is *Tiger*, latest of the "Splendid Cats" and the largest warship to take part in the First World War.

Lion was flagship of the battle cruisers throughout the war and took part in both the Battles of Dogger Bank and Jutland. She was badly mauled at the Dogger Bank, receiving 17 hits and being put out of action. Beatty transferred his flag to *Tiger*, but owing to muddles in signaling, the British failed to follow up his squadron's initial success in sinking *Blücher* and allowed the rest of the enemy to escape.

At Jutland *Lion* was again badly damaged, but in spite of a nearly disastrous long-range hit from *Lützow*, she survived and led the British battle cruisers to the end of the battle.

internal protection concentrated attention on the need for improved subdivision and for better distribution of deck protection and internal longitudinal bulkheads.

The British government, as part and parcel of the switch to oil, bought a controlling share in the Anglo-Persian Oil Company. Only in 1987 did the privatization of BP (British Petroleum, the new name of the company) bring this stake to an end. Abādān on the Tigris became in due course the world's largest oil refinery; the Royal Navy's supplies were secured, and it received them at a concessionary price.

Queen Elizabeth, completed in 1915, was the very pinnacle of Dreadnought technology: powerful, fast, battle worthy. She also had a balance of line that had been lacking from her predecessors: magisterial seems the best term. She was the first of a class of five, and they were so good that they proved worthy of adaptation to meet the needs of a very different type of warfare 25 years later.

The second ship, *Warspite*, bore a time-honored name. For the third ship, Churchill proposed the name Oliver Cromwell, but King George V disapproved, suggesting *Valiant* instead. The fourth was named for Admiral Barham and the fifth for the Federated States of Malaya, which had raised the funds for her construction by popular subscription.

As soon as she was commissioned, *Queen Elizabeth* was sent to the Mediterranean, where it was thought that her long-range guns would be effective in reducing the Turkish forts within the Dardanelles.

In fact, the attempt to shell targets on the east shore of the Gallipoli Peninsula by firing blindly over the intervening high ground proved ineffectual, partly due to lack of faith in the credibility of gunnery spotting from aircraft.

She was absent from the Battle of Jutland, although her four consorts, who formed the 5th Battle Squadron, played a critical role in the battle. She was chosen by Admiral Beatty to become his flagship when in 1916 he succeeded Jellicoe as Commander-in-Chief of the Grand Fleet. *Queen Elizabeth*, therefore, took pride of place on November 21, 1918, when the Fleet sailed out to meet the surrendering ships of the German High Seas Fleet.

It was an event without historical parallel. Under the terms of the Armistice, the principal part of the German Navy was to land its ammunition and the breechblocks from its guns and to sail within seven days across the North Sea to surrender. Mutinous crews had formed revolutionary committees on board the ships, and only with the greatest difficulty was the command able to exert sufficient discipline to comply. The sullen, neglected-looking ships steamed out to sea for the last time in a light morning mist. They were to be met by a British light cruiser and led towards the Firth of Forth. Forty miles off the coast, they sailed into an overwhelming display of armored force: 370 ships of the Grand Fleet, manned by 90,000 men.

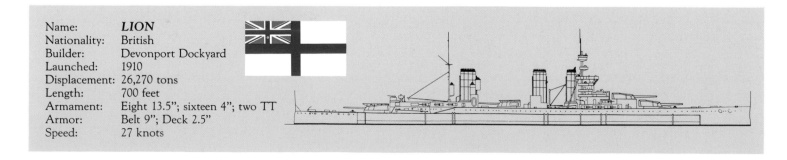

Name:	*LION*
Nationality:	British
Builder:	Devonport Dockyard
Launched:	1910
Displacement:	26,270 tons
Length:	700 feet
Armament:	Eight 13.5"; sixteen 4"; two TT
Armor:	Belt 9"; Deck 2.5"
Speed:	27 knots

The Grand Fleet was deployed in two parallel lines, six miles apart, and they stretched as far as the eye could see. There were no less than 46 battleships and battle cruisers, including a squadron of American battleships. All ships were cleared for action, and crews stood to their guns.

As they came abreast of the German fleet, the whole force wheeled, squadron by squadron, to take up station on either flank. The entire parade passed May Island and entered the broad expanse of the Firth, where the ships dropped anchor.

It was a spectacle such as would never be seen again, but it was a moment of tragedy, not cheap triumph. In four years of war, the profligate expenditure of lives and of valor had drained the ardor of all the belligerents, and it brought about social revolution in four empires.

In the years between the two world wars, *Queen Elizabeth* was reconstructed twice. Bulges were fitted to the sides of the hull to improve her underwater protection and more armor was provided against aerial attack. Her anti-aircraft armament was increased, and a hangar, catapult, and cranes were fitted to enable her to launch and recover her own aircraft. Her appearance was completely transformed.

During the Second World War, she served in the Mediterranean and in the Indian Ocean. In December 1941 she and her sister ship *Valiant* were badly damaged while lying in Alexandria Harbour by Italian frogmen who planted limpet mines. Both ships were repaired and survived the war. *Queen Elizabeth* later took part in operations against the Japanese in Burma and in the Andaman Islands.

Warspite became notorious for getting herself into trouble. At the Battle of Jutland, her steering jammed as a result of being put hard over at 25 knots, and she made two involuntary circles in the face of the enemy, suffering severe damage. In April 1940 she took part in the attack on German forces at Narvik,

which resulted in the sinking of ten destroyers. She was Admiral Cunningham's flagship in two encounters with the Italian navy in the eastern Mediterranean, and she was present at the surrender of the Italian Fleet in 1943. *Warspite* was damaged by bombing off Crete in 1941, very nearly sunk by a radio-controlled bomb off Salerno in 1943, and struck a mine in the North Sea later in the war. Nevertheless, she survived hostilities and ended her career by breaking her tow on the way to the ship-breakers and being wrecked on the coast of Cornwall. Some said it was characteristic of the old lady.

The ships of the *Queen Elizabeth* class played an important role for 30 years, and they exerted an influence on world events far beyond the measure of the resources devoted to their construction.

CHAPTER X

THE BATTLE OF JUTLAND

Twice, and only twice, throughout the era of the armored ship whole fleets of battleships clashed and locked together in a pitched battle. The first occurred in May 1905 when Rozhestvensky's weary ships finally confronted the nimble Japanese that they had steamed so far to meet. The second took place on the last day of May 1916, when Admiral Jellicoe led the Royal Navy into battle with the Kaiser's High Seas Fleet.

In the First World War, the British strategy was very simple: to blockade the coast of Germany and deny the country the means to wage war. Of course there were other contributions and other theaters, but Britain never supposed that its army would be large enough to have much impact on the land war in Europe.

Conventional wisdom held that a blockade should be maintained by ships stationed close off the enemy shore. This is the way it had always been done. Only in 1912 had the Naval Staff secretly decided that now it should impose a distant blockade, with the main fleet based at the northern point of access to the North Sea. The critical new factor was the effectiveness of mines, submarines, and torpedoes, which meant that passage of the English Channel could be denied to enemy surface ships. On the other hand the same weapons in enemy hands rendered the maintenance of a close blockade off the German-held coastline extremely dangerous. This was vividly demonstrated when six weeks after the outbreak of war, a German submarine sank three armored cruisers within 45 minutes, close off the coast of Belgium.

The main force of the Royal Navy was held at Scapa Flow in the Orkney Islands, poised to support the blockading cruisers that patrolled the 200-mile-wide entrance to the North Sea. German trade with the world was stopped, and the possibility of German interference with British shipping, with the passage of reinforcements, or with her freedom of action in any part of the oceans was completely denied while this blockade was maintained.

It slowly dawned on the Germans that the close blockade on which their plans were based was not going to be put into effect. The hope of whittling down the British superiority in numbers of big ships by a constant process of harassing with mine and torpedo could not be realized. They were obliged to try to draw out the British ships by making raids on the east coast of England, hoping to entice a portion of the fleet into action where it could be outnumbered. They were successful in causing the Royal Navy to station its battle cruisers further south, from whence they could retaliate more quickly.

The Royal Navy was superbly confident. The Grand Fleet was named for the fleet that had been mustered under Howard, Frobisher, and Drake to do battle with the Spanish Armada. Attention was focused on gunpower; comparisons with foreign ships were invariably on the basis of the relative weight of their broadsides. To prevent the enemy from getting away, speed was essential, but the risk of being sunk through lack of protection was not a high priority. There is evidence that shutters designed to prevent the spread of flash between turret, hoist, handing rooms, and magazines had been removed by gunnery officers anxious to improve their own ships' rate of fire in competition with others at maneuvers.

The German High Seas Fleet was inferior that day in numbers, in weight of gunpower, and in speed. But German battleships, ship for ship, were better armored, beamier, and more fully subdivided internally. The fleet was a sharp-edged weapon, skillfully trained, with superior optical range finders and better armor-piercing shells. The danger from burning cordite in a turret had been revealed by a disastrous fire in *Seydlitz* during an engagement four months previously, so all German ships had been equipped with improved anti-flash protection. The Germans had also trained to fight by night. Instead of relying on labored codes in Morse, colored recognition lights in the rigging could be flashed on, and star shell was employed to illuminate the enemy without revealing a ship's location.

The German Commander-in-Chief, Admiral Scheer, planned to bombard Sunderland on May 17 in order to lure out the battle cruisers and then to spring on them before the main battle fleet could reach the scene. Part of the plan involved laying an ambush of submarines off the battle cruiser base in the Firth of Forth. The operation depended on reconnaissance by Zeppelins to ensure that the Grand Fleet itself was not at sea. Bad weather made this impossible, so the Admiral substituted a more modest plan in which his ships would not venture far from the west coast of Denmark.

Alerted of Scheer's movements by the wireless traffic heard by the Admiralty, the British under Admiral Jellicoe regarded the German sortie as a long-sought opportunity to bring the enemy to decisive action.

Jellicoe sailed from Scapa Flow with 24 battleships; Admiral Beatty departed from the Firth of Forth with six battle cruisers and four of the new fast battleships. Both fleets would converge on a rendez-vous south of the southern tip of Norway. With all the accompanying cruisers and destroyers, it was a fleet of unprecedented size: some 150 ships and 60,000 men. German forces were four-fifths as many.

Each fleet had its battle cruisers out ahead; each side was unaware that the other's main battle fleet was at sea. Cruisers made contact at 2:15 p.m., shortly before the British were due to join forces. Mindful of earlier frustrations, Beatty tore off to intercept. Admiral Hipper, commander of Scheer's Scouting Group, obediently turned for base in order to lead the British unsuspectingly into the guns of the High Seas Fleet.

At 3:45 began the first phase, the Run to the South. The weather was misty, the wind in the northwest. Beatty's six wicked-looking battle cruisers were outlined against a brighter horizon, their funnel smoke and cordite interfering with their gunners' aim. Beatty, with an edge in speed and guns of greater range, had the option of keeping his distance, but he allowed Hipper to close the range. The German shooting was superb. In a gun duel lasting an hour, the German battle cruisers inflicted far more damage than they sustained.

After 15 minutes Beatty's flagship *Lion* was hit by a shell that peeled open the roof of the midships turret, igniting charges of cordite. Prompt action by the mortally wounded turret officer, who closed the doors and flooded the magazines below, was alone responsible for preventing an explosion that could have destroyed the ship. The last ship in line, *Indefatigable*, was hit by a salvo of three 11" shells from *Von de Tann* at more than 22,000 yards. Plunging at the limit of their trajectory, the shells pierced the armored deck and exploded deep inside. The battle cruiser staggered out of line, and a second salvo, half a minute in flight, descended onto the foredeck. A cordite flash reached a magazine, and with a tremendous roar the ship disappeared in vast

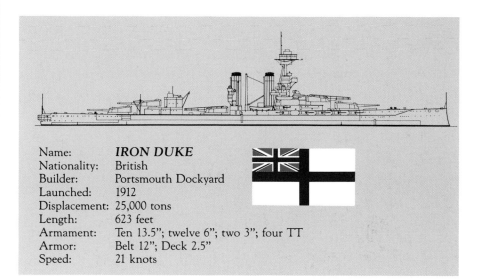

Name:	**IRON DUKE**
Nationality:	British
Builder:	Portsmouth Dockyard
Launched:	1912
Displacement:	25,000 tons
Length:	623 feet
Armament:	Ten 13.5"; twelve 6"; two 3"; four TT
Armor:	Belt 12"; Deck 2.5"
Speed:	21 knots

Plate 38.

IRON DUKE

Malta, 1924

The battleship was a visible token of power. In the era of the armored ship, no place on earth was more resplendent with the power of battleships than Grand Harbour, Malta.

Captured from the French in 1800, Malta provided Britain with a naval base at the crux of the Mediterranean, equally accessible to east and west. The island was small enough to be easily defended, but the harbor was big enough to shelter a fleet, which could watch the whole coastline of southern Europe, France, Italy, Austria, and the Levant.

The deepwater inlets of Grand Harbour's magnificent setting are dominated by the great sandstone ramparts built by the Knights of St. John. The mighty warships lay incredibly close to the shore, and walking through the streets of Valletta one would suddenly glimpse their towering funnels and mastwork glittering in the sun at the end of some narrow, shaded alleyway. On the far side of the harbor are a series of fortified headlands, separated by creeks, the most prominent of which is Fort St. Angelo.

Iron Duke was the name ship of a class of four Dreadnoughts completed in 1914; she became Admiral Jellicoe's flagship on his appointment as commander of the Grand Fleet and served thus at the Battle of Jutland. In 1919 she was posted as flagship of the Mediterranean Fleet.

Iron Duke's signal flags are in naval code, which indicates, "Usual leave may be granted to officers."

billows of smoke. When the battleship *Malaya*, hastening to catch up with the battle cruisers, passed through the flotsam minutes later, the crew cheered because they were so sure that it must be the wreckage of a German ship.

Minutes later the *Queen Elizabeth*-class fast battleships began to come into range with their mighty 15" guns, and they threw up taller splashes with the others around Hipper's ships. Distrusting wireless, which was apt to break down under concussion, Beatty had relied on flag signals, and difficulty in reading these had led to the *Queen Elizabeth*s being left behind. At 4:26 another of Beatty's ships blew up. Two German ships were firing on *Queen Mary*, sharply etched against the western sky, when a salvo of four shells struck the British ship together, causing a terrific explosion. A mushroom of smoke rose a thousand feet, and the two ships following her in line passed through a ghastly shower of falling debris. As her stern reared out of the water with the propellers still slowly revolving, a cloud of papers was seen fluttering out of the after hatch.

More than a thousand men died.

Beatty's famous remark to his flag captain, "Chatfield, there seems to be something wrong with our bloody ships today," sums up the cool assurance that nevertheless pervaded the fleet. British gunlaying steadily improved, and now that the four battleships were coming up behind, the battle cruisers forged ahead and turned 45 degrees toward the enemy to cut them off from their base. The British Admiral ordered destroyers to launch a torpedo attack, which was countered by German destroyers. A frenzied and heroic battle took place between the lines. One German battle cruiser was hit by a torpedo, and two destroyers were lost by either side.

At this juncture Beatty's scouting light cruisers reported the electrifying news of the approach of the main German battle fleet. The tables were turned. Now it was Beatty's job to lure the whole High Seas Fleet northward and deliver it into the arms of Jellicoe's battle fleet.

By this stage the wireless on *Lion* was out of action, and again the *Queen Elizabeth*s failed to read her flags. They overshot the battle cruisers as they spun around to a northern course. Just as Togo's ships at Tsushima had done, the four British battleships turned in succession, each passing through the same spot, and the last one received a fearful hammering from concentrated German fire.

Fortunately they were tough, and Admiral Scheer's three leading battleships were damaged in their turn. During the Run to the North, the British began to inflict severe punishment on the enemy battle cruisers. *Von der Tann* was silenced, *Derfflinger* was badly hit, and *Seydlitz* came close to foundering. German shellfire seemed to make no impression on the *Queen Elizabeth*s.

The speed of Beatty's battle cruisers was unimpaired. As they drew near the battle fleet, Beatty had to prevent Hipper from sighting Jellicoe's ships in time to warn Scheer. Drawing ahead, but still bombarding Hipper with his 13.5" guns, which had the range, Beatty forced his adversary to turn farther and farther to the east.

Jellicoe was 50 miles to the north when he received

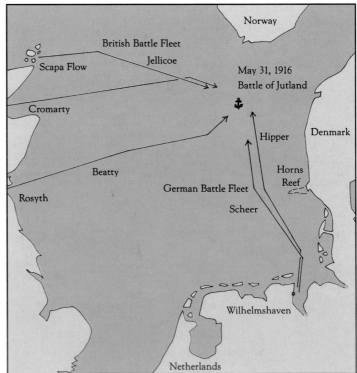

**Jutland
The setting**

Norway

British Battle Fleet
Jellicoe

Scapa Flow

May 31, 1916
Battle of Jutland

Cromarty

Hipper

Denmark

Beatty

Horns
Reef

German Battle Fleet

Rosyth

Scheer

Wilhelmshaven

Netherlands

the report of Beatty's scouting cruiser at 4:30. Just after 6:00 the battered *Lion* was sighted by the flagship, tearing up from the southwest and trailing a long, ragged plume of black smoke. Gathering mist mingled with the smoke of battle had reduced visibility to six miles, and there was barely three hours of daylight left.

Flickering signal lamps enquired desperately the bearing and course of the German battle fleet. Beatty could not say.

Jellicoe would never have a second chance. Everything depended on the right choice now. He had to form the whole compact mass of British battleships into a line to bring them, if possible, across the enemy's bows. After a moment's deliberation he settled for deployment behind the port column, ship by ship and column by column, reducing speed as the battleships majestically took up station.

Beatty's line was joined at the head by three fresh battle cruisers, which had been based in the Cromarty Firth and had arrived with Jellicoe's fleet. Hipper began to wonder if the supply of enemy ships was endless.

One of these ships, *Invincible*, was the original of all battle cruisers. By a trick of the weather, she appeared to Hipper's ships suddenly out of the mist, racing through a fleeting patch of sunlight. A salvo of shells was immediately directed on her. Once more the dreadful spectacle of a great armored ship exploding took place as *Invincible*'s magazines detonated by cordite flash from several hits. The ship disappeared in a mighty cloud. Bow and stern stood up out of the water for more than half an hour, resting on the shallow bed of the sea. It was a macabre sight.

At 6:30 the two battle fleets finally made contact. To lookouts in the Grand Fleet, the German heavy ships began to show up one after the other through shrouds of mist and smoke, outlined now and then against the lighter southern horizon. Hipper's burning battle cruisers led the full panoply of Scheer's High Seas Fleet: 16 Dreadnoughts followed by six older battleships. This time the British had the advantage of wind and light.

To Scheer, the reality of his predicament was

The night of May 31, 1916

Plate 39.

KONGO

Kure, 1928

The Japanese battle cruiser *Kongo* is seen here at Kure Navy Yard. In the background lies her sister ship *Kirishima*; in the distance, the battleship *Yamashiro*.

This view shows well the lithe and powerful appearance of the *Kongo*-class ships as they looked when first built. The characteristic shape of the four British-pattern, twin 14"-gun turrets, the closely spaced tripod masts, and the ripple of 6"-battery casemates along the main deck below forecastle deck level are very noticeable. The forward guns were closely superimposed, but the after turrets were spaced widely apart in order to permit super-firing directly astern and to minimize the chances of a single hit affecting both turrets.

Kongo was the last of a long series of capital ships built for the Imperial Japanese Navy in British yards, and the first battle cruiser. She formed the model for three sister ships, which were built in Japan. For more than 20 years, they remained among the fastest capital ships in the world. Twice reconstructed in the years between the wars, they were lengthened and obtained new machinery and additional armor. All four saw hard service in the Second World War. *Kongo* was sunk by the U.S. submarine *Sealion* in 1944.

abruptly revealed. It was he who had been led into a trap. The horizon from northwest to northeast was obscured by smoke, but it sparkled with the muzzle flashes of an enormous arc of British guns.

The situation was critical. Every German ship simultaneously turned through 180 degrees, reversing their order in line, as well as their direction. The evolution had been well practiced and it was carried out without a hitch. Six minutes after Jellicoe sighted the German battleships, the High Seas Fleet disappeared into the gloom.

Jellicoe, baffled at the first moment, decided not to follow. He had recorded his opinion months before that such a turn away was likely to be intended to lead his ships into an area sown with mines. Instead he directed the fleet southward, to cut off the enemy from the German base.

Hipper, in the meantime, was searching for a suitable flagship. He had been forced to abandon *Lützow* in sinking condition. Boarding a destroyer he tried *Derfflinger*, *Seydlitz*, and *Von der Tann*; each ship in turn proved to be too badly disabled, and it was 10:00 that night before he was able to hoist his flag in *Moltke*.

Now as dusk drew in, Scheer ordered another reversal of course. While his reasoning is obscure, it seems he supposed that the British line would by now have passed to the south. Between 7:10 and 7:18 the High Seas Fleet ran straight back into that great arc of gun flashes from which it had so recently been extricated. This time the range was much closer and the hail of fire more damaging.

Once again Scheer ordered an instant turn about. To cover the battle fleet, the battle cruisers were to be sacrificed in a headlong dash toward the enemy line. The battered German ships were in no condition to do more, and within a few minutes they were recalled, reeling under shellfire from ranges down to 8,000 yards. Scheer's retirement was covered by a massed destroyer attack, which caused the Grand Fleet to turn away. Surprisingly, the torpedoes could be seen when they were up to two miles away, enabling ships to steer to avoid them.

Jellicoe's squadrons turned back to the southwest in pursuit of the enemy. By 8:23 the leading battle cruisers caught up with Hipper's ships again and began inflicting further damage. In response Scheer ordered his six old pre-Dreadnoughts, whose loss would not be serious, to relieve the battle cruisers, but by now it was becoming too dark for effective gunnery.

The Royal Navy was tense with anticipation; the fleet was disposed, in overwhelming strength, between the German ships and their home base. All that was needed was to renew the action at daybreak in order to achieve the decisive victory to which it was so obviously entitled.

Jellicoe had long decided to avoid night actions. Experience at night exercises had demonstrated how risky they could be, and the one thing to avoid at this stage was a gamble. Jellicoe confidently anticipated victory on the first of June.

Two choices appeared to lie before the Germans. They could continue south, close to the coast of Holland, and try to double back to port behind the protection of minefields. Or they could take a direct line for the mouth of the Jade, with the risk of again running into the Grand Fleet.

Jellicoe decided that the former was the more likely. Therefore, he carried on the course just slightly east of south. His line of ships stretched for 25 miles, and there was a good chance that it would bar the way to any attempt by Scheer to break through during the few short hours of darkness. But the Germans were well equipped for night fighting, and Scheer unhesitatingly chose the direct route home. His ships were in no condition to reopen the action the next day, and he cut smartly across the rear of the British line, reaching the

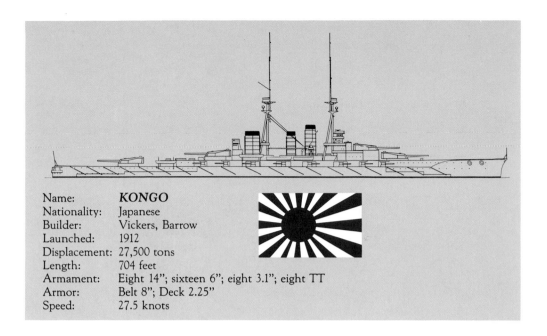

Name:	**KONGO**
Nationality:	Japanese
Builder:	Vickers, Barrow
Launched:	1912
Displacement:	27,500 tons
Length:	704 feet
Armament:	Eight 14"; sixteen 6"; eight 3.1"; eight TT
Armor:	Belt 8"; Deck 2.25"
Speed:	27.5 knots

entrance through the minefields at 3:00 a.m.

Scheer's fleet did not pass unnoticed. Frantic, desperate actions between individual ships took place in the darkness as the German fleet passed the rear of the line. The British were bewildered and uncoordinated. A series of savage encounters took place; British destroyers made two gallant torpedo attacks, sinking one battleship, and cruiser forces clashed with several losses.

The Germans reached the safety of the swept channel by the skin of their teeth. Only by the narrowest of margins did Hipper's four remaining battle cruisers make it home. (*Lützow* sank in the night.) Several times heavy units were seen by individual British battleships, but they were allowed to get away again in the darkness.

Recriminations were exchanged for years to account for the British failure to intercept. Intelligence passed on by Room 40 at the Admiralty was disgracefully misused, individual captains failed to take initiatives, and Beatty always believed that his own advice had been neglected. The fact remains that opportunity slipped through Jellicoe's fingers.

In the aftermath of battle, each side concentrated on getting its damaged ships home. A British minefield skillfully laid in the swept channel of the Jade claimed but a single victim, and that ship, a pre-Dreadnought battleship, was able to reach port. German submarines could not be reached by wireless; those patrolling off the Forth had given up and turned for base.

When they reached Scapa Flow, the ships of the Grand Fleet were rebunkered and replenished. Within three hours Jellicoe routinely reported that the fleet was again fit for sea.

The situation on the other side of the North Sea was very different. The ships and crews of the High Seas Fleet were in shattered condition. Those who had experienced the holocaust never forgot it. Two years later when a massive German offensive blundered to a halt on the Western Front, the call came to commit the fleet in a last throw to reverse the tide of war. When ordered to sea in October 1918, the ships' companies doused their boiler-room fires.

The fundamental outcome of the Battle of Jutland was that nothing had changed. The stranglehold maintained by the Royal Navy was never relaxed for a day.

Mutiny in the navy precipitated civil insurrection in Germany, but ultimately four years of unremitting blockade had brought about the conditions of national collapse.

Plate 40.

ALMIRANTE LATORRE
Gulf of Peñas, Chile, 1929

The climax of the South American Dreadnought race was the order placed by Chile in 1911 with Armstrong of Elswick for two battleships that would outclass their Argentine and Brazilian counterparts. The ships, still under construction at the outbreak of war in Europe in August 1914, were bought by the British government. The first, *Almirante Latorre*, was not far from being ready for sea; she was completed and named *Canada*. Construction of her sister ship, *Almirante Cochrane*, was much less advanced.

She was eventually completed in 1920 as the aircraft carrier *Eagle*.

Canada, which served throughout the war in the Grand Fleet, took part in the Battle of Jutland. She was delivered to the Chilean Navy after being refitted in 1920 and served nearly 40 years as flagship of the fleet before finally being retired in 1958.

Almirante Latorre is pictured against the heroic backdrop of snowy mountains and glaciers in the Gulf of Peñas, a thousand miles south of Valparaiso. In the background

lies the old armored cruiser *General O'Higgins*, also built by Armstrong and completed in 1897.

Her flags read YD2, which is evidently the battleship's recognition signal; the Chilean Navy employed Roval Navy code flags.

CHAPTER XI
THE RISING SUN IN THE WEST

In the years leading up to 1914, America watched with growing concern the creation of a large modern navy by Japan. In April 1915 the Japanese armored cruiser *Asama* became stranded on a sandbank at Turtle Bay in Baja California, located on the inner coastline of the Mexican peninsula. *Azuma* stood by with other units to tow *Asama* off; both ships were veterans of the Battle of Tsushima. What were they doing there? It transpired that Japan was in negotiation with Mexico for the establishment of naval facilities on the west coast, and there were rumors of even more sinister intentions.

The incident did not pass without notice in Berlin. German agents had been active in stirring Mexican resentment of the U.S. intervention at Veracruz, for nothing would be more convenient than to have the United States become embroiled in a guerilla war in Mexico. The German navy eyed the use of submarine bases in the Gulf. General Huerta, the exiled Mexican dictator, arrived in New York to plot a return to power with German help, and he very nearly accomplished this before being stopped just short of the border.

Count Zimmermann, the German foreign minister, saw the opportunity of exploiting American apprehensions about a Japanese-Mexican alliance to distract the United States from coming to the aid of France and Britain. In particular the growing pressure in Germany to resume unrestricted submarine warfare seemed to him certain to precipitate American entry into the war, and anything should be done to try and forestall that event.

On January 16, 1917, Zimmermann sent a telegram to the German ambassador in Mexico. The ambassador was to inform the Mexican government that in the event of American entry to the war, Germany proposed an alliance with Mexico and Japan, in which Germany would provide financial support and uphold Mexico's claim to recover the lost territories of Texas, New Mexico, and Arizona. In the absence of any direct means of communication, the coded message, incredibly, was sent through U.S. diplomatic channels, ostensibly as part of the negotiations conducted by President Wilson in an effort to bring an end to the war. The telegram was transmitted along the submarine cable via London, where it was intercepted by the British Admiralty.

The sequence of events that followed is worthy of novelist John Le Carré. The British had broken the German code, but the message was so outrageous that the Admiralty decided the Americans would never believe it.

They set about finding corroboration. This they eventually achieved by securing another text of the same message sent via Sweden and by stages through German agents in several South American countries. When all the evidence was eventually set before President Wilson, the Zimmermann telegram finally exhausted even his patience and led to the American declaration of war.

During the period 1910 to 1918, America set about constructing a massive force of armored ships. By 1919 the pace had become furious. In that year Japan and the United States between them were building 12 Super Dreadnoughts and had authorized

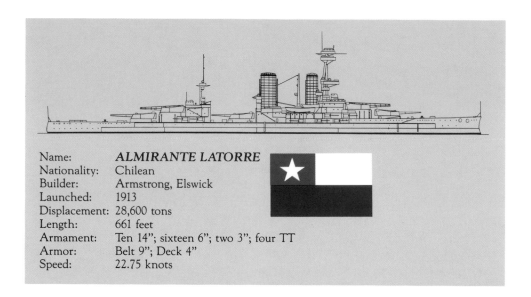

Name:	**ALMIRANTE LATORRE**
Nationality:	Chilean
Builder:	Armstrong, Elswick
Launched:	1913
Displacement:	28,600 tons
Length:	661 feet
Armament:	Ten 14"; sixteen 6"; two 3"; four TT
Armor:	Belt 9"; Deck 4"
Speed:	22.75 knots

20 more. The United States, to its eternal credit, called an international conference on Naval Disarmament.

The outcome of the Washington Conference stabilized the status quo. The Royal Navy was no longer preeminent. Britain, in her supreme exertion to overcome the German war machine, had drained herself of gold, of men, and of energy. Plans had been laid in Britain to build more mighty ships to match those of America and Japan, but the country had neither the means nor the will to do so. At some point in the middle of the First World War the balance of worldwide power had slipped from Britain to the United States.

The Conference agreed to freeze the size of the three principal navies—American, British, and Japanese—in the ratio 5:5:3. In the following years America was able with confidence to place her principal naval strength at Hawaii; she no longer had to be concerned about the possibility of confronting a European naval power.

The prospect of naval operations across the vast expanses of the Pacific called for a new emphasis on speed and range, and a special interest in aerial reconnaissance. Naval aviation had been pioneered during the war, largely by Britain. Seaplanes had been used to launch torpedoes successfully against shipping as early as 1915, and carrier-borne aircraft had effectively attacked Zeppelin bases on land. By the end of the war, the ships of the Grand Fleet carried more than 100 aircraft on their turrets when they put to sea, this in addition to the planes that were accommodated in the fleet's four makeshift aircraft carriers. The first true flattop, *Argus*, joined the Royal Navy within a few weeks of the armistice. After the war Japan eagerly adopted British doctrine and embarked on a serious program of building and training a naval air arm. America, too, within a few years overtook Britain in devoting resources to the construction of aircraft carriers and the development of naval aircraft types.

Japan was obliged to recognize that it had neither the financial strength nor the industrial facilities to enable it to outbuild the U.S. Navy. The Washington Treaty was legalistic confirmation of harsh reality. Nevertheless, America had shown itself always ready to obstruct Japan in its boldest ambitions, and the United States was regarded as the potential antagonist.

Japan turned to wit and wile to provide the advantage that could not be achieved by weight of numbers. The wit was directed toward developing

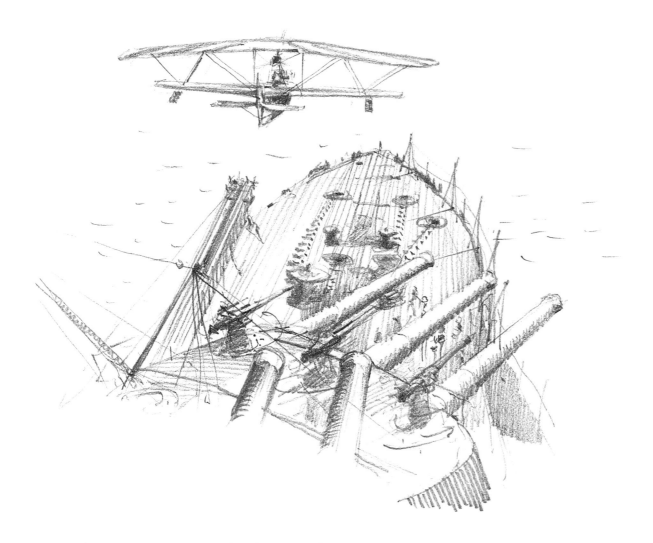

and perfecting new weapons and techniques of naval warfare. The wile was to wrap a veil of secrecy about equipment and intentions.

The aircraft carrier, with its shipboard torpedo-carrying planes and dive bombers, was not the only new technique. The Japanese pinned great faith in newly developed long-range torpedoes that had a speed of 48 knots. These missiles, which could outrange 16" guns, traveled without leaving a conspicuous wake. Fast light cruisers were converted to carry them in large numbers. Such ships were intended to attack the enemy at night before the main encounter between battle fleets took place. The Japanese planned to launch 230 torpedoes from ranges of up to 35,000 yards.

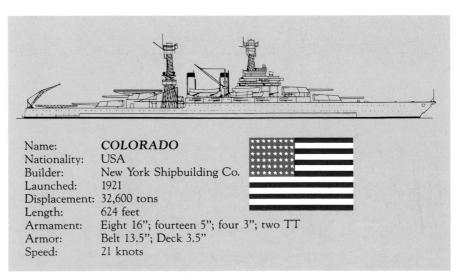

Name:	**COLORADO**
Nationality:	USA
Builder:	New York Shipbuilding Co.
Launched:	1921
Displacement:	32,600 tons
Length:	624 feet
Armament:	Eight 16"; fourteen 5"; four 3"; two TT
Armor:	Belt 13.5"; Deck 3.5"
Speed:	21 knots

Plate 41.

PENNSYLVANIA

East River, New York, 1936

The battleship *Pennsylvania* has just emerged from Brooklyn Navy Yard and is about to pass beneath the Brooklyn Bridge. She is being assisted by a bustling collection of New York tugs. In the background can be seen the slender towers of the Wall Street area at the extremity of downtown Manhattan as they appeared before being crowded by massive new buildings in the 1970s.

Pennsylvania, which had been built in 1913-16, was reconstructed in the late 1920s and presents a very different appearance

from when she was first completed. Two large catapults had been installed: one fixed on the roof of Number 3 turret, and one pivoted on the quarterdeck. Each catapult carries two Curtiss SOC-1 Seagull Scout Observation biplanes.

During the attack on Pearl Harbor, *Pennsylvania* was in dry dock. She was therefore secure from attack by torpedoes and was hit by only a single bomb, which caused little damage.

When the United States returned to the

Philippines in October 1944, *Pennsylvania* and five older U.S. battleships took part in the Battle of Surigao Strait. This proved to be the last occasion on which battleships engaged each other at war.

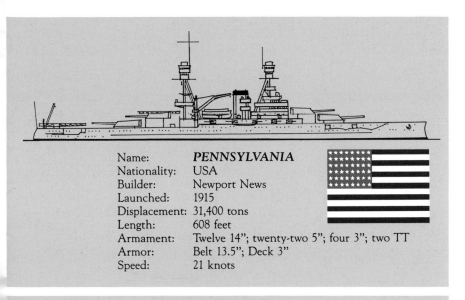

Name:	**PENNSYLVANIA**
Nationality:	USA
Builder:	Newport News
Launched:	1915
Displacement:	31,400 tons
Length:	608 feet
Armament:	Twelve 14"; twenty-two 5"; four 3"; two TT
Armor:	Belt 13.5"; Deck 3"
Speed:	21 knots

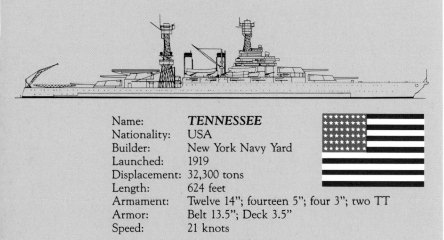

Name:	**TENNESSEE**
Nationality:	USA
Builder:	New York Navy Yard
Launched:	1919
Displacement:	32,300 tons
Length:	624 feet
Armament:	Twelve 14"; fourteen 5"; four 3"; two TT
Armor:	Belt 13.5"; Deck 3.5"
Speed:	21 knots

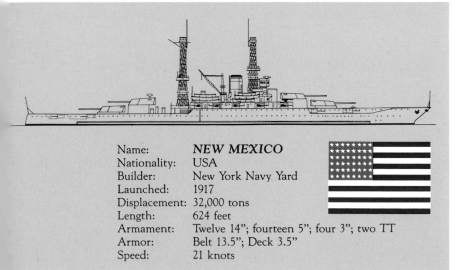

Name:	**NEW MEXICO**
Nationality:	USA
Builder:	New York Navy Yard
Launched:	1917
Displacement:	32,000 tons
Length:	624 feet
Armament:	Twelve 14"; fourteen 5"; four 3"; two TT
Armor:	Belt 13.5"; Deck 3.5"
Speed:	21 knots

The most important new weapon was, curiously, a type of armored ship, for the Japanese still considered that the decisive encounter would be a gunnery duel. In 1937 they set out to build the *ne plus ultra* of battleships. Once more, the old idea recurs: quality would be brought to outweigh an inescapable shortfall in quantity.

The plan was to build ten giant ships between 1936 and 1946 and to rearm them successively with yet bigger guns. In this way the Japanese intended to maintain superiority for a period of ten years.

In the event, only two of these monster ships were completed, and a third was converted to an aircraft carrier. The first, *Yamato*, went into service one week after the attack on Pearl Harbor.

Secrecy enshrouded all aspects of construction. Enormous curtains of sisal rope were erected around the slipways where they were built, and the size of their guns was a forbidden topic. Only after the end of the Second World War did the true facts become known outside Japan. The battleships displaced more than 70,000 tons, and their guns were of 18" caliber, with a range of 27 miles. Shells fired by such guns weighed 50 percent more than the 16" projectiles of the *Iowa* class.

The biggest secret of all was the decision to make an unprovoked attack on Hawaii. The American fleet, like the Russians at Port Arthur, was to be reduced in one great preemptive strike before the start of war.

The attack was devastatingly successful. But the appalling scene masked the vital fact that not one of the American aircraft carriers had been present. By default, the carriers became the principal arm of the U.S. fleet, and six months later they broke the power of Japanese naval aviation at the Battle of Midway.

Ironically, the Japanese had diverted much of their precious resources to the construction of armored prodigies. The super-battleships proved to be dinosaurs; the armored ship had been overtaken by evolution.

Plate 42.

TENNESSEE

Charlestown, Boston, 1937

Tennessee is seen slipping out to sea from Charlestown Navy Yard, Boston, one morning in 1937. In the background is the Customs House Tower in the financial district; in the distance lies South Boston, and on the left are the wharves of East Boston.

Tennessee and her sister ship *California* mounted their secondary armament of 5" guns in casemates on upper-deck level instead of at main-deck level as in earlier battleships. This enabled the guns to be worked in heavier seas and improved the watertight integrity of the ship. Another pair of guns was mounted one deck higher still, but without protection, on the same level as the eight 5" anti-aircraft guns.

On the large catapult mounted on the roof of Number 3 turret sit two Curtiss SOC-3 float biplanes used for gunnery spotting.

Tennessee, at Pearl Harbor during the Japanese attack, escaped serious damage, due to having been moored inboard of *West Virginia*. During 1942 she was extensively rebuilt, which completely altered her appearance, and thereafter she took part in many of the island bombardments in the course of the Pacific campaign. She was present at the Battle of Surigao Strait; later she was engaged in operations in the East China Sea, off Shanghai and against Okinawa.

CHAPTER XII

THE WHITEHEAD TORPEDO

Robert Whitehead, a British engineer working with an Austrian naval officer, Commander Luppis, produced at Fiume in 1864 the first workable torpedo. The difficulty had been to find an effective means of control, and this was finally achieved by the use of water pressure to trim horizontal fins and a gyroscope to maintain direction. Whitehead brought his device to Britain, but it took many years to develop a weapon of sufficient speed, range, and reliability to fulfill early expectations. Nevertheless, the torpedo exerted a profound effect on naval policy, and for a time many thought that the days of the large armored ship were numbered.

Small, fast craft termed torpedo boats were designed for launching the missiles; as with rockets in our own day, the launching device could be quite light and simple compared with the vessel required for mounting heavy guns. The first torpedo boat was built by Thorneycroft in 1876, and although such flimsy craft had limited endurance and could operate only in sheltered waters, they began to be regarded as a serious threat to armored ships.

In response, big ships were armed with machine guns, small quick-firers, and searchlights; provided with steel torpedo nets that could be swung out on booms from the sides of the ship; and greater attention was paid to the design of underwater subdivision. In France the introduction of torpedo warfare was greeted, like the explosive shell and the armored ship, as another new technique with which to offset Britain's superiority in numbers of conventional warships.

France concentrated on building a large force of torpedo boats, but practical experience in annual maneuvers failed to confirm their effectiveness. The boats were unseaworthy, and the torpedoes were too restricted in range and speed. The first use of a torpedo in action, when the British steam frigate *Shah* launched one against the rogue Peruvian ironclad *Huascar*, ended humiliatingly when the target outran the pursuit.

French officers of the so-called *Jeune Ecole* during the final quarter of the nineteenth century advocated the employment of torpedo craft, submarines, and commerce raiders against British trade, rather than attempt to match the Royal Navy's fleet of armored ships.

French policy wavered, however, and a rapid succession of Naval Ministers brought about constant changes of construction policy. As in the United States, there were some who pinned their faith in shallow-draft armored ships for coastal defense and some in large armored cruisers for commerce destruction.

Battleships continued to be added to the fleet, and the strength of the French navy was never greatly inferior to that of the British before 1885. It was recognized that without a battle fleet the coast of France would be subjected to blockade, individual raiders would be gradually but inevitably eliminated, and overseas possessions would be at the mercy of their enemy.

The design of French armored ships was quite distinctive. They favored high freeboard and, to

Plate 43.

ARIZONA

San Francisco, 1937

Arizona follows three other battleships of the Pacific Fleet out of San Francisco Bay on maneuvers. They are about to pass under the great span of the Golden Gate Bridge; opened in May of 1937, it was by far the longest single span in the world.

Arizona and *Pennsylvania* were completed in 1916, closely resembling the preceding pair *Oklahoma* and *Nevada* but with twelve 14" guns instead of ten. All four ships were modernized in the years 1926 to 1929 in order to fit them with anti-torpedo bulges and to

rid them of their conspicuous cage masts.

Sixteen battleships were built for the U.S. Navy between 1910 and 1921, and many of them saw service in both world wars. Over the years great changes were made to their appearance, and those that survived the disaster of Pearl Harbor were subsequently rebuilt so extensively that they came to look like new ships.

Nine of these older U.S. battleships were at Pearl Harbor on December 7, 1941, and all were damaged in the attack. Three ships

were brought back into service within four months, three were salvaged and rebuilt, and three— *Arizona*, *Oklahoma*, and the target vessel *Utah*—were destroyed beyond recovery. The wreck of *Arizona* still lies on the seabed, where it has been dedicated to the 2,300 sailors who died on that day, many of them in *Arizona*.

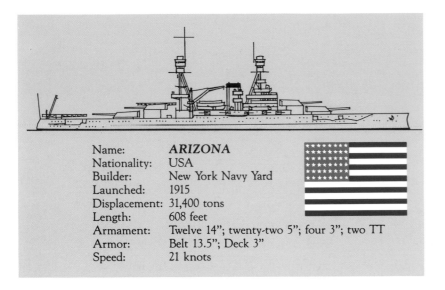

Name:	**ARIZONA**
Nationality:	USA
Builder:	New York Navy Yard
Launched:	1915
Displacement:	31,400 tons
Length:	608 feet
Armament:	Twelve 14"; twenty-two 5"; four 3"; two TT
Armor:	Belt 13.5"; Deck 3"
Speed:	21 knots

gain stability, exaggerated tumble home (much greater beam at the waterline than at the level of the deck). Another reason for adopting this hull form was to provide a better field of fire for guns mounted on sponsons at the sides of the ship. The armored belt was a narrow one close to the waterline, leaving a large expanse of the ship's side unprotected, and the hull was vulnerable to hits below the waterline. The French favored a full-length belt and protective deck rather than limiting armor to vital areas.

French armored ships were hardly ever tried in action, but French-built battleships were used by the Russians, and Russian ships were built to French design. In the Russo-Japanese War they stood up well to the test of action. They proved to be extremely difficult to sink by gunfire; battle damage might look bad, but the vitals of the ship were often unaffected. The shock of the war was the disastrous effect of mines on the armored ships of both sides.

Early torpedo boats were designed to be hoisted on board armored ships in order to bring them closer to the scene of action, but the process of launch and recovery was cumbersome.

Instead, torpedo boats tended to get larger. One impulse for this was the evolution of torpedo boat destroyers as a means of countering the threat of torpedo boat attack. Destroyers were larger and more heavily armed, but they were no slower than their prey, and they too carried torpedo tubes. On account of their greater seaworthiness and endurance, they proved more useful than torpedo boats and gradually displaced them for fleet use.

By the 1880s it had become normal practice for armored ships themselves to mount torpedo tubes. The practice was universal until well into the 1920s, although no record seems to exist of torpedoes fired successfully by a heavy ship in action.

Naval tactics were heavily influenced by the prospect of attack on a battle fleet by destroyers or submarines and by the possibility of heavy ships firing torpedoes or laying mines in their wake.

The fears and expectations for torpedoes were a long time in being fulfilled. Up to the 1940s torpedoes were not outstandingly reliable, they were little faster than their targets, and they left a track which could be seen and avoided. Battleships were designed with heavier and heavier secondary and tertiary armaments to defend themselves against destroyers, and only at night or in restricted waters did attacks on alert and well-handled heavy ships stand any chance of success.

Torpedo attacks were carried out by destroyers of both sides at the Battle of Jutland; they were pressed home with tremendous dash and gallantry, but the one battleship sunk by this weapon was attacked at close range in the confusion of the night. At the Battle of Tsushima, torpedo boats were only sent in at the end of the day when their targets were already disabled and many were stationary in the water.

For success with torpedoes it was essential to get close, and an able commander would not neglect to screen the fleet with destroyers and light cruisers in order to keep this kind of assailant at arm's length. The deadly potential of the torpedo was fulfilled in attack by submarines and later in the launching of these weapons from aircraft. In two World Wars less than a dozen battleships were sunk by torpedoes fired by submarines, but a great many more were damaged, and fleet operations in both wars were heavily circumscribed by the constant threat of underwater attack. The Royal Navy was petrified of submarines in the opening phases of World War I, before its base at Scapa Flow was given protection, and the nightmare materialized when *Royal Oak* was sunk within the fleet anchorage in October 1939. It was, however, the aerial-launched torpedo that proved to be the nemesis of the armored ship.

Before the outbreak of the Second World War, it was obvious that aircraft would play a major role in naval operations. Land-based aircraft seriously constrained the use of warships in the North Sea and the Mediterranean, and they inflicted many losses on cruisers and destroyers that were operating beyond the range of their own air cover.

The first successful air attack on capital ships took place in November 1940, when a handful of torpedo-carrying aircraft from the aircraft carrier *Illustrious* raided the main Italian fleet base at Taranto. The attack was carried out by Swordfish biplanes, which were slow by comparison with land-based types, so the attempt was staged at night.

The raid was a startling success. Three battleships were torpedoed and sunk. The fact that they were lying in shallow water enabled two of the ships to be salvaged, including the new battleship *Littorio*. Nevertheless, the immediate effect was to halve the strength of the Italian fleet. Only two aircraft were lost.

In March 1941 *Littorio*'s sister ship *Vittorio Veneto* encountered the British Mediterranean Fleet under Admiral Cunningham south of Crete. The British included the carrier *Formidable*, which launched

three attacks with her Albacore aircraft on the Italian battleship. One torpedo hit *Vittorio Veneto*, causing serious damage, but she was able to recover sufficiently to achieve half speed and made good her escape. The heavy cruiser *Pola* was also hit, and two sister ships were detached to stay behind and assist her. The Royal Navy, unlike the Italians, was equipped with radar, and during the night Cunningham's ships stole up on the three big cruisers. Suddenly illuminating the scene with searchlights, the British force of three veteran battleships smothered the enemy with 15" caliber shellfire. The execution was brief and complete, and three heavy cruisers and two destroyers were sunk within minutes.

Aircraft launched from the carrier *Ark Royal* played a critical role in the chain of events leading to the destruction of *Bismarck*, for it was a single torpedo hit on the German battleship that brought her to bay. Other attempts on capital ships from the air were less successful; torpedo planes failed to stop *Scharnhorst* and *Gneisenau* passing through the

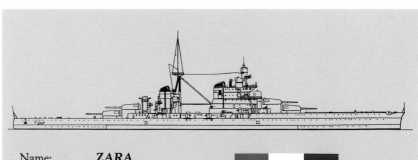

Name:	**ZARA**	
Nationality:	Italian	
Builder:	Odero-Terni, La Spezia	
Launched:	1930	
Displacement:	13,580 tons	
Length:	624 feet	
Armament:	Eight 8"; sixteen 3.9"	
Armor:	Belt 6"; Deck 3"	
Speed:	32 knots	

Plate 44.

HOOD and *BARHAM*

Grand Harbour, Malta, 1938

Hood, which is just getting under way in the restricted waters of Bighi Bay, was in her day the world's largest warship, with a displacement of 43,000 tons. Because of her size, speed, and impressive appearance, she was highly esteemed in public opinion, but by the outbreak of the Second World War, the mighty battle cruiser was 20 years old and due for modernization. Her destruction by *Bismarck* in 1941, with the loss of almost her entire crew, was regarded as a national disaster.

The battleship *Barham* in the background is flying the flag of the Commander-in-Chief, Mediterranean Fleet. She is one of five *Queen Elizabeth*-class ships, all of which were extensively modernized in the 1930s. She saw service at the Battle of Jutland in 1916, at Dakar, and at the Battle of Cape Matapan in March 1941. In November 1941 she was sunk off the coast of Egypt by three torpedoes fired by the German submarine U331.

Roysterer, in the foreground, is a twin-funneled Admiralty tug built in 1918.

In the Royal Navy turrets were described, from the bow, as A, B, Q (amidships), X, and Y. The broad red, white, and blue stripes painted on the roofs of B and X turrets were recognition marks applied during the Spanish Civil War to prevent ships of the international patrol from being bombed by belligerents.

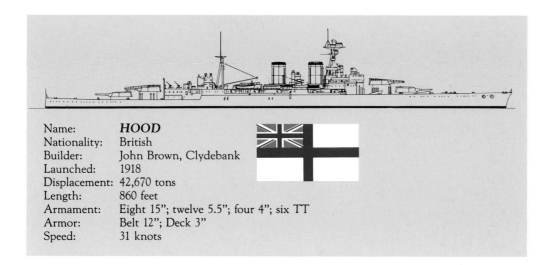

Name: **_HOOD_**
Nationality: British
Builder: John Brown, Clydebank
Launched: 1918
Displacement: 42,670 tons
Length: 860 feet
Armament: Eight 15"; twelve 5.5"; four 4"; six TT
Armor: Belt 12"; Deck 3"
Speed: 31 knots

English Channel, and in one attack on _Bismarck_ by aircraft from _Illustrious_, a torpedo hit on the armored belt of the battleship had precisely no effect at all. Nevertheless, carrier-borne planes successfully disabled the French battle cruiser _Dunkerque_ as she lay aground after the bombardment of Mers-el-Kébir, and others seriously damaged the battleship _Richelieu_ at Dakar.

Torpedoes carried by British aircraft were small ones, 18" in diameter instead of 21", and the damage caused by a single hit was often not conclusive.

No doubt the operation at Taranto was closely observed in Japan. One Sunday morning 12 months later, 335 carrier-borne aircraft descended on Pearl Harbor. Nine major armored ships and two cruisers were sunk or severely damaged, although because they were sunk in shallow water, it proved possible to salvage most of them in due course.

Three days later came the sinking of two British capital ships at sea off Malaya by Japanese land-based aircraft.

Thereafter heavy armored ships became subordinate in naval operations. The war in the Pacific evolved as a contest between carrier forces, supported and protected by big-gun ships.

The final and conclusive blow to the concept of the armored ship was delivered by aircraft. American carrier-borne planes sank the two greatest battleships ever built: _Musashi_ and _Yamato_. Designed to survive the heaviest gunfire, these Japanese warships succumbed to massive assaults by bombers and torpedo-carrying aircraft.

In October 1944 during the battle to oppose the American return to the Philippines, _Musashi_ was subjected all day long to attacks from the air. Only after she had received no fewer than 19 hits from torpedoes, coupled with damage from 10 bombs, did the enormous vessel gradually fill with water, capsize, and sink.

Five months later her sister ship _Yamato_ was dispatched from mainland Japan in a desperate attempt to interrupt the landings on Okinawa. She too was overwhelmed by great numbers of aircraft, rather more than had been employed by the Japanese for the attack on Pearl Harbor. There was little to oppose them, and after receiving more than ten torpedo hits, she sank, taking with her most of her crew of 2,500.

After this, no nation would build more armored ships.

Plate 45.

ZARA and *FIUME*

Genoa, 1938

With a long extended coastline on two sides of the country, the Italian navy had an unenviable task of defense. Unable to match her likely antagonists in numbers, she tended to build ships that were faster than those of other navies and also, in many cases, ships more heavily armed. The Italian aim was to seek action only under favorable circumstances. Italian armored ships were all classed as *Navi da Battaglia* rather than as battleships and cruisers; the concept of the line of battle had no place in Italian strategy.

From 1929 to 1931 four 8"-gun cruisers of the *Zara* class were laid down at Italian yards. Their 6" armored belts and 3" decks provided heavier protection than that of contemporary foreign cruisers, and their speed was 32 knots. (*Zara* achieved 34.2 knots on trials.) Two aircraft were carried in a hangar in the bow. Surely the most handsome cruisers ever turned out, the four Italian ships made a great impression at maneuvers in the 1930s, including a display carried out for Hitler off Naples in 1938.

This picture depicts two of the class off the renowned maritime city of Genoa, with the cranes of the famous Ansaldo shipyard visible in the background beyond *Fiume*.

On March 28, 1941, three of the *Zara*-class cruisers came to grief at the Battle of Cape Matapan.

Plate 46.

ADMIRAL GRAF SPEE
Montevideo, 1939

Germany's decision to build new armored ships in the 1930s was the subject of bitter controversy at home and generated apprehension abroad. The ingenuity of their design caused serious concern in Britain, for the Germans seemed to have achieved the long-sought objective of every privateer: speed capable of outpacing a more powerful adversary coupled with strength enough to crush any lesser. The new technique of welding rather than riveting saved weight, and diesel propulsion conferred tremendous

cruising range. The German government, seeking to reassert the nation's place in the world, bragged of the pocket battleships' potency as commerce raiders.

Panzerschiffe, as they were known, were to be the naval counterpart of the Blitzkrieg, the combination of weapons (tanks and dive bombers) and technique (speed and mobility) that was to overwhelm enemies on land.

All the more striking, therefore, was the humiliating failure of *Admiral Graf Spee* to withstand the aggressive tactics of three not-

so-large British cruisers. In October 1939 she took refuge in Montevideo, Uruguay, after an inconclusive action with *Exeter*, *Ajax*, and *Achilles*.

In the picture one of the British cruisers waiting anxiously offshore has sent over her Fairey Seafox float plane to try to see what damage *Admiral Graf Spee* has sustained. The German ship did not emerge to confront the cruisers again; she was scuttled by her crew on direct orders from Hitler.

CHAPTER XIII

ARMORED CRUISERS AND PANZERSCHIFFE

The frigate was a smaller version of the principal type of warship, the line-of-battle ship. Its functions were to act as scout and messenger, as commerce raider or convoy escort, and generally to act independently of the main force of the fleet. Of similar rig and general layout to line-of-battle ships, frigates were considerably faster and carried only a single deck of guns.

The line-of-battle ship had two or three gun decks, and she was rated according to her number of guns. First, second, and third rates carried, say, 90, 74, or 54 guns (there were variations over the years), whereas frigates mounted 30 to 40 lighter weapons. No frigate could expect to stand up to a ship-of-the-line.

The battle fleet could not be everywhere, nor could it remain at sea indefinitely without the absence of individual ships for repair and revictualing. So even a superior fleet experienced great difficulty in maintaining a continuous blockade on a lesser fleet or on a long coastline. Frigates were employed to extend the range of surveillance.

During the Anglo-American War of 1812 the British were heavily extended in their prolonged struggle against Bonaparte in Europe. A few frigates were regarded as sufficient to contain the newly created U.S. Navy. What the British failed to appreciate was that the first three frigates that had been built to start that navy were especially powerful ships. The creation of a fleet of line-of-battle ships was beyond the needs or the resources of the new country, but the frigate *Constitution* and her sisters were much larger, more heavily built, and far

more heavily gunned than normal frigate practice. Furthermore, the new republic was by no means short of experienced manpower, (the population was more than half that of Britain at that time), and the ships were ably manned and commanded. Three stinging encounters in the opening year of the war, each of which resulted in the defeat of individual British frigates, caused consternation in the hitherto unassailable Royal Navy.

Thus marked the beginning of a story of evolution in warship design outside the main stream. The heaviest fighting ships were designed to overcome the principal enemy fleet in a general engagement, but actions outside the main theater called for different qualities, particularly speed and endurance.

During the American Civil War, the Union with superior forces was able to exert a naval blockade on the ports of the South. The Confederate navy resorted to worldwide commerce raiding as a means not only to damage Union trade but to draw off naval forces from their blockading function.

At the beginning of the war, the Southern command recognized the leverage that would be gained by the use of armored ships against a wooden navy, and, lacking the resources to build such ships, it sent a purchasing mission to Europe.

Unsuccessful in its attempt to purchase the world's first ironclad, *La Gloire*, the mission managed to arrange the surreptitious construction of about two dozen vessels in England and France. The governments of both countries seized some of the newly built ships and were able to prevent the delivery of others, but the British-built raiders *Florida* and

Name:	*ADMIRAL GRAF SPEE*
Nationality:	German
Builder:	Wilhelmshaven Naval Yard
Launched:	1934
Displacement:	13,750 tons
Length:	610 feet
Armament:	Six 11"; eight 5.9"; six 4.1"; eight TT
Armor:	Belt 4"; Deck 1.75"
Speed:	28 knots

Alabama both sailed under the Confederate flag. The best known, *Alabama*, was a fast screw frigate, only moderately armed and lacking armor. In the course of a spectacular career, she captured 69 prizes before being sunk by the Union steam frigate *Kearsarge* off Cherbourg.

The only armored ship to evade the authorities was *Stonewall*, built in Bordeaux. She was delivered too late to take part in the war, but her fighting power overawed the Union warships sent to shadow her across the Atlantic. She was eventually bought by the Shōgun of Japan, seized by the Japanese Emperor, and served in the Imperial Navy for 20 years.

The Union responded to Confederate commerce raiders by constructing a class of large iron screw-propelled frigates with a limited armament of heavy-caliber guns.

In the nineteenth century Britain, with her scattered possessions overseas and her growing dependence on worldwide seaborne trade, was becoming more and more exposed to the threat of commerce raiding. To counter this, larger types of frigate were also introduced in the Royal Navy. The type evolved into the iron- or steel-masted cruiser, the protected cruiser, and eventually into the armored cruiser.

It was many years before sailing rig could be discarded for ships that had to keep to the sea for prolonged periods and to serve on distant stations, but it proved difficult to combine sailing rig with speed under steam. As late as 1889 one cruiser on maneuvers was able to outstrip pursuing warships by hoisting "all plain sail." The design of cruisers diverged; the larger types were provided with steel protective decks near the waterline and some with vertical armored belts, and the smaller types concentrated on speed. The latter were characterized by the *Iris* of 1877, a British steel-built twin-screw vessel whose hull was packed with machinery. Her sailing rig was vestigial, good only for emergencies, but the yacht-like cruiser could make 18.5 knots under power. She was the forerunner of the twentieth-century light cruiser: slim, fast, and dashing.

The other category of cruiser properly forms part of the story of the armored ship.

Armored cruisers in the nature of small-scale battleships were built for the Russian, French, and British navies in the 1870s. Displacing about 6,000 tons, they were armored with a vertical belt of 9" thickness on the waterline and a protective deck. But such ships were no faster than contemporary battleships, and their usefulness was open to doubt.

The Italian navy, looking mainly towards France as a likely antagonist, sought to offset Italy's smaller financial and industrial resources by building individual ships of greater power and speed. As with the first American frigates, the objective was to outmatch any one opponent and to be able to escape from a superior force.

Following this policy Italy produced in the course of 40 years several generations of innovative warship designs. Her naval architects Benedetto Brin and Vittorio Cuniberti led the way in many developments, but the country's limited shipbuilding capacity resulted in long construction times.

First came *Duilio* and *Dandolo*, completed in 1880. They were turret ships with giant 17" guns

Name:	**WARSPITE**
Nationality:	British
Builder:	Devonport Dockyard
Launched:	1913
Displacement:	31,315 tons
Length:	639 feet
Armament:	Eight 15"; eight 6"; eight 4"; thirty-two 2-pounder
Armor:	Belt 13"; Deck 5"
Speed:	23.5 knots

supplied by Armstrong and with correspondingly heavy protection. They appeared to be so powerful that the British felt obliged to build a ship specifically to meet them on equal terms. Five years later Benedetto Brin produced *Italia* and *Lepanto*. The four big guns were this time mounted in open barbettes mounted well above water level on a hull with generous freeboard, and armor protection was sacrificed to speed. The ships were designed to carry troops and land them at any point on Italy's long coastline that might be subjected to enemy attack. In this the Italians foreshadowed the specialized ships designed for amphibious warfare in recent times.

The sequence of Italian shipbuilding was continued by Cuniberti's *Regina Elena* of 1907. Faster than any existing battleship, she had a mixed main armament of 12" and 8" guns, all mounted in turrets, and could be regarded as the precursor of the battle-cruiser concept. Next came the extraordinary *Dante Alighieri* of 1913. Long and low, with four widely spaced triple 12" turrets, her two groups of twin funnels were spaced towards either end of the ship. The design sacrificed protection in the search for superior speed and firepower.

None of these designs was ever tested in action, and in the First World War, Italy was eventually drawn in on the side of France and Britain. No encounter took place with the Austrian fleet.

The French naval architect Emile Bertin designed a ship that worried the British. She was a 6,500-ton armored cruiser called *Dupuy de Lôme*, which was completed in 1891. Intended as a commerce raider, this long vessel with high freeboard and armament of two 7.6" and six 6.4" guns was completely protected by 4" vertical side armor, backed by a 2" thick armored deck, and she could achieve a speed of 20 knots. The widely spaced groups of funnels and the extreme tumble home of her sides were characteristic of French design. This ship set the pace for a whole series of French and then of Russian cruisers of increasing size, range, and potential. Though aimed primarily at self-preservation from their common antagonist in central Europe, the Entente concluded between France and Russia obliged Britain to face the possibility of meeting their combined navies in war. Shipbuilding was accelerated to meet what was described as the Two Power Standard.

During the last quarter of the nineteenth century, more than 100 cruisers were built for the Royal Navy, all of them protected by an armored deck, but only a few were given an armored belt. Their roles were to protect trade, to chase and destroy raiders, and to act as scouting groups in advance of the main battle fleet. Representative of these was *St. George* of the *Edgar* class of 1892. On a displacement of 7,700 tons, she mounted two 9.2" guns fore and aft, ten 6", and made a speed of 18.5 knots. She had a 5" deck but no vertical armored belt. We have met her before at Zanzibar.

The need for ships able to tackle powerful raiders such as *Rurik*, built by Vickers for the Russian navy and delivered in 1896, led to ever larger protected cruisers. Eventually the armored cruiser idea was

Plate 47.

WARSPITE
Narvik Fjord, 1940

During the German invasion of Norway in April 1940, it was reported that one party of troops had landed at the port of Narvik in the far north of the Scandinavian country. A British force of five H-class destroyers was sent to penetrate up the long and tortuous Westfjord leading to Narvik, with orders to sink the ships that had landed the troops.

The troop transports turned out to consist of ten large destroyers of the *Karl Galster* type. A violent battle, which took place in a snowstorm, resulted in two of the German destroyers being sunk and five being damaged. The British lost two ships and sustained damage to one other as they retired to the open sea.

Three days later the Royal Navy returned to finish the job. Admiral Whitworth boldly entered the confined waters of the fjord with the battleship *Warspite*, screened by a force of nine destroyers. A Walrus flying boat catapulted from the battleship reported the enemy's positions and also succeeded in sinking a submarine by bombing.

As *Warspite* steamed ponderously up through the narrowest part of the fjord, the thunder of her 15" guns echoing and reverberating between the high rock walls was described as awe-inspiring.

In the course of an hour's engagement, the eight remaining German destroyers sought refuge in the remotest headwaters of the fjord, but one by one they were all destroyed. Two *Tribal*-class destroyers accompanying *Warspite* were damaged.

Plate 48.

STRASBOURG

Mers-el-Kébir, Oran, 1940

Fifty years after the French surrender to the Germans in 1940, it is not easy to evoke the tense atmosphere in Britain, which had every reason to expect invasion within weeks. The armistice signed on June 22 between Hitler and Pétain permitted France to retain control of her navy, but Britain was justifiably skeptical. Two years later the German army did not hesitate to march into unoccupied France and attempt to seize the fleet.

When the armistice was signed, the main part of the French fleet was at Mers-el-Kébir in Algeria. On July 3 British Admiral

Somerville arrived off the port with a strong force to present the French with an ultimatum. Either the French could join the British in continuing to fight the Germans, place their ships under British control, or sail with reduced crews to Martinique. If these options were all rejected, the French were to sink their ships within six hours.

French Admiral Gensoul refused to negotiate, and when the time limit expired, Somerville was obliged to open fire. No commander was ever placed in a more disagreeable situation, for there were many

British who had personal friends on the other side.

In the course of a 15-minute bombardment, the old battleship *Provence* was badly damaged and beached, *Bretagne* blew up and capsized, and *Dunkerque* was crippled and ran aground. The modern battle cruiser *Strasbourg* alone managed to get under way and escape from the harbor undamaged. Attempts to sink her by aircraft from the carrier *Ark Royal* were unsuccessful, and she reached Toulon safely the next day.

revived. Characteristic of the type was *Good Hope*, completed in 1902. She was a big ship, longer than a battleship, and displaced 14,000 tons. She had a 6" armored belt and a speed of 23 knots, but within a few years she was eclipsed by a new class of armored ship.

The big Russian cruisers that had been such a concern to the British were based at Vladivostok in 1904. At the Battle of Ulsan, the three ships were tackled by four Elswick-built Japanese armored cruisers with 8" guns; *Rurik* was sunk, one was disabled, and the other Russian cruiser was badly damaged.

At this point the development of cruisers took a new twist, for the revolution in design of battleships precipitated by Admiral Fisher in 1906 was accompanied by a fresh approach to the issue of large cruisers. Parallel with development of the Dreadnought battleship, work was initiated on what was at first termed the Dreadnought cruiser.

The reasoning behind the development of the Dreadnought cruiser was that a larger margin of speed and gunpower was needed to catch and sink commerce raiders of growing size and power, and at the same time the scouting force of the battle fleet should be equipped to outreach an enemy reconnaissance group and prevent its approach to the battle fleet. Thus the idea for a ship of great size and speed germinated. It would be armed with big guns equal in range and caliber to those carried by battleships, and all would be achieved at the expense of armor protection and secondary armament. The battle cruiser, as it became known, would use speed as its protection.

For bravura there was nothing like it. The first battle cruiser, *Invincible*, was completed in 1908. She was long and lean with a high freeboard, an armament of eight 12" guns all mounted in turrets, and three spaced-out funnels. Her top speed was a sensational 26.5 knots. At a stroke, all the big armored cruisers were rendered obsolete.

The pace of technical innovation over the next eight years was fast and furious. Five more "I"-class battle cruisers followed *Invincible*, but by the outbreak of war in Europe in 1914, they had been dangerously outmoded. Each year saw improvements in gunpower, speed, and protection of battle cruisers. *Invincible* acquitted herself handsomely, however, when she was sent off with one of her colleagues to deal with Graf Spee's victorious cruiser squadron in the South Atlantic.

Germany was the first nation to follow suit, developing her own design of battle cruiser with rather less striking power and much improved protection. In the scramble for superiority, battleships were soon built with the speed of battle cruisers, and battle cruisers became no less well armored than battleships. The armored ship had evolved by 1919 in a spectrum that ranged between the long, fast, and relatively lightly protected vessels and the broader, slower, more heavily armed and armored types. The term capital ship was coined to cover all.

Cruisers, in the meantime, evolved in their own direction. Speed was paramount, and offensive power was augmented by deck-mounted torpedo tubes in addition to the guns. Armor was generally limited to relatively light protective decks.

The genealogy of armored ships includes one curious branch of the family. An outcome of

Name:	**STRASBOURG**
Nationality:	French
Builder:	St. Nazaire, Penhoët
Launched:	1935
Displacement:	25,500 tons
Length:	704 feet
Armament:	Eight 13"; sixteen 5.1"; eight 1.5"
Armor:	Belt 9.5"; Deck 3.6"
Speed:	29.5 knots

Fisher's myopic enthusiasm, the so-called large light cruisers of the *Glorious* class completed in 1917 were larger, faster, and flimsier than any capital ship of the day, and they carried just four 15" guns. Too much emphasis was laid on a particular hypothetical role, and in war the unexpected often takes place. Nevertheless, the *Glorious*-class cruisers were potentially supreme commerce raiders, and their design did not pass without notice in Europe.

One of the provisions of the Washington Treaty on Disarmament of 1921-22 limited the size of cruisers to 10,000 tons and armament to 8" guns. Given the agreed-upon restrictions on capital ships, all the major naval powers felt obliged to proceed with construction of big cruisers of this type. It was a rerun of the armored cruiser story.

Britain elected, as before, to take the route of developing well-armed ships with only a protective deck and a reasonable turn of speed. The Italians, again, built ships with dazzling performance and characteristics that on paper appeared incontestable.

American interwar 8" gun cruisers were superior in armament and protection to the British. The Japanese, who kept everything secret, were later discovered to have produced by far the most potent ships.

Germany, which took no part in the Washington Conference, was limited in naval construction by the Treaty of Versailles. Under its terms she was permitted by 1928 to start adding to her navy warships of up to 10,000 tons.

Armored ships were regarded by many as symbolic of militarism and reeking of the chauvinism that had marked the period leading up to the First World War. To some, a warship was a much more visible and tangible token of military power than, say, a regiment of infantry. Others in Germany, however, saw the construction of such ships as necessary to the reassertion of national dignity. The decision to lay down the first new armored ship was therefore the subject of bitter controversy in the

Reichstag before authorization was finally approved. Her name was *Deutschland*, and her design concept was extremely ingenious.

Panzerschiffe, as she and her sister ships were termed, were direct descendants of the large commerce-raiders of 30 years before. The British press described them derisively as pocket battleships, but the term was not inapt. They mounted two triple turrets of 11" guns, plus a secondary armament of eight 5.9" and a battery of torpedo tubes. One feature that belonged to their own generation was the accommodation of seaplane aircraft for scouting. The armored belt was not substantial, and the most unusual aspect of their design was the machinery, a combination of diesels and turbines that conferred great endurance coupled with high emergency speed. Only seven ships in the world had the speed to catch them and an armament superior in range; they were the three surviving British battle cruisers constructed during the First World War and the four Japanese veterans of the *Kongo* class. Only long afterwards was it revealed that the pocket battleships far exceeded the treaty limit on displacement.

Germany followed the first three *Panzerschiffe* with two larger vessels, *Scharnhorst* and *Gneisenau*, and all five ships conducted successful commerce raiding operations in the opening years of World War II.

The final chapter in the armored cruiser story concerns one of the pocket battleships, christened with prescience *Admiral Graf Spee*.

Operating in the South Atlantic in October 1939, the the German ship was tracked down by wireless transmissions from one of her victims. Three British cruisers made contact with her off the mouth of the River Plate.

Exeter, an 8"-gun Washington Treaty cruiser, had three instead of the usual four twin turrets. The others, *Ajax* and *Achilles*, were typical light cruisers with eight 6" guns. *Achilles* was a member of the

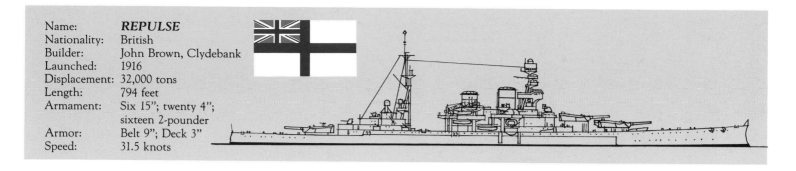

Name:	**REPULSE**
Nationality:	British
Builder:	John Brown, Clydebank
Launched:	1916
Displacement:	32,000 tons
Length:	794 feet
Armament:	Six 15"; twenty 4"; sixteen 2-pounder
Armor:	Belt 9"; Deck 3"
Speed:	31.5 knots

New Zealand armed services.

The balance of forces was delicate. *Admiral Graf Spee* could outrange her opponents and could not easily be injured by 6" shellfire, unless by a lucky hit. On the other hand, there were three of her opponents, and they were faster. Skillfully dispersing his forces, Commodore Harwood forced *Admiral Graf Spee* to divide her fire, but she was not to be distracted and scored seven hits with 11" shells on *Exeter*. All three of the lightly built British cruisers harried the big armored ship in spite of the superior weight of the German ship's fire. A Fairey Seafox float plane was launched from *Ajax* to help with spotting the fall of shot, and at two points in the action, the British cruisers fired torpedoes, but these were seen and avoided by the pocket battleship. After an hour *Exeter*'s guns were silenced, and she was obliged to break off the action. The 6"-gun cruisers pressed on to closer range, attempting to inflict at least some damage on the pocket battleship. *Achilles* was slightly damaged, and in *Ajax* the two after turrets were put out of action. At this point the cruisers turned away with the intention of renewing the attack under cover of darkness.

During the engagement, *Admiral Graf Spee* had received 18 hits by 8" and 6" shells, most of which caused seemingly trivial damage. A number of 6" shells had struck the armored belt or the fronts of gun turrets and simply ricochetted into the sea, but even minor damage was a very serious matter for a ship that was isolated so far from home.

The splinters sent out by all these hits had caused,

when taken together, a considerable amount of damage to the ship's fire-control and radio equipment and a large number of casualties. Captain Langsdorff, the commander, was wounded, though not seriously.

With the enemy's fighting capacity apparently undiminished, the British were surprised to find themselves following a ship that seemed bent on escape. Langsdorff had decided to head for a neutral port to carry out repairs. *Exeter*, meanwhile, was in very serious condition and in no state to rejoin action with the enemy.

Commodore Harwood's two remaining cruisers were fired at several times by the larger ship, but they escaped without further damage and closed up as night fell and *Admiral Graf Spee* entered the wide estuary of the River Plate. The bay is 120 miles wide, and the deep water channels are divided by several shoals. Harwood must have been reluctant to divide his puny force, but he was even more concerned that the enemy would elude him. His ships were not equipped with radar.

The pocket battleship put in to the roadstead of the Uruguayan capital of Montevideo on the north shore of the estuary. Under the Hague Convention of 1907 a combatant is permitted refuge in a neutral port for 24 hours, after which the ship is to be interned for the duration of hostilities. Captain Langsdorff estimated that he needed 14 days to effect the necessary repairs to enable his ship to fight its way through the North Atlantic. The critical damage was mostly in the form of leaks in the hull

Plate 49.

QUEEN ELIZABETH

Suez Canal, 1941

A close-up view shows the great battleship towering over the streets of Port Said as she passes through the canal. On completion of her reconstruction in early 1941, she was assigned to the Mediterranean. In December of that year, three Italian two-man submarines penetrated the defenses of Alexandria Harbor and succeeded in attaching limpet mines to the hulls of several ships. *Queen Elizabeth* and her sister ship *Valiant* were both seriously damaged. Sunk in shallow water, *Queen Elizabeth* was quickly raised, received tem-

porary repairs, and then made her way to Norfolk Navy Yard, Virginia, for permanent repairs. The extent of her damage was successfully concealed from the Italians.

It is interesting to compare this view with one of the same ship passing under the Forth Bridge in 1916 (Plate 35). In the years between the First and Second World Wars, *Queen Elizabeth* was twice reconstructed, receiving new propulsion machinery, "bulges" on the sides of the hull, a dual-purpose 4.5" secondary armament, and air-

craft handling equipment. Her two funnels were trunked into one, and her tripod foremast was replaced by a massive architectural bridge structure. At one point during the war, the battleship passed the Cunard liner *Queen Elizabeth* in mid-Atlantic. Both ships smartly hoisted the signal SNAP.

and an unexploded shell that needed to be extracted.

The British, of course, were feverishly trying to assemble a force of warships off the coast of South America to deal with *Admiral Graf Spee*, but the battle cruiser *Renown* and aircraft carrier *Ark Royal* were more than 3,000 miles away, a distance of five days' steaming. The only immediate reinforcement was the 8"-gun cruiser *Cumberland*, which was pounding northwards from the Falklands. She carried eight guns to *Exeter*'s six, but she was no more heavily armored. If *Admiral Graf Spee* emerged next morning, she would face only the two light cruisers.

But she did not emerge. Langsdorff was granted an additional stay of 72 hours by the government of Uruguay on the grounds that his ship was unseaworthy. He attended the funeral of 37 of his men, who were killed in action, and arranged for hospitalization of the wounded. Later that day he received reports from the German Embassy in Buenos Aires, across the river, that *Ark Royal* and *Renown* were approaching the Estuary of the Plate, and a private plane chartered by the Embassy reported sighting four British cruisers off the river mouth. *Admiral Graf Spee*'s Arado 196 float plane had been damaged in the action, but a nervous gunnery officer in the ship's director control tower reported seeing through the lenses of the range finder a large warship, which he considered to be the *Renown*, and an aircraft carrier and destroyers on the horizon.

The following day Harwood, now reinforced by *Cumberland*, sent aloft his float plane to try to make out what *Admiral Graf Spee* was up to. On land there was a flurry of diplomatic activity. The Germans wanted to stave off internment in Uruguay at all costs and considered the possibility of making a dash across the river to Argentina. The British were anxious to delay the ship's departure until the arrival of heavier forces, so they arranged for the sailing of a British merchantman from Montevideo, which under international law meant that *Admiral Graf Spee*'s departure had to be postponed for a further 24 hours.

Langsdorff was assailed by a variety of rumors, some well-intentioned and some inspired, indicating the concentration of naval forces off the mouth of the river. The time limit expired at 8:00 p.m. on the fourth day, and at 6:15 p.m. the pocket battleship weighed anchor.

It was a Sunday, and enormous crowds lined the Prado, the breakwaters, and the shoreline as the German ship hoisted all her battle flags and stood out to sea. There was eager anticipation of being able to watch a naval battle from the shore. Overhead, a float plane circled to observe the proceedings. The pocket battleship suddenly veered out of the main channel and towards the west, apparently heading for Buenos Aires. Then she steered into shoal water and anchored once more.

Just as the setting sun touched the horizon, the remaining crew were taken off, and ten minutes later the ship was obliterated by a great flash followed by a billowing plume of black smoke from a magazine explosion. The event was well recorded; many will remember the extraordinary newsreel photographs of the burning wreck and the curiously rubbery-looking remnants of twisted steel hull and upperworks.

Captain Langsdorff took his own life.

Plate 50.

REPULSE

Kilindini Harbour, Mombasa, 1941

The rakish battle cruiser *Repulse* slips into Kilindini Harbour, Mombasa, en route to Singapore. In the foreground is the ramp to Likoni Ferry, which connects Mombasa Island with the south mainland.

Repulse was built on the Clyde in 1915-16. She mounted six of the big new 15" guns and could do more than 31 knots. Extensively reconstructed from 1933 to 1936, she was given additional armor and anti-aircraft guns, and aircraft hangars with a cross-deck catapult were installed amidships. One of her Supermarine Walrus flying boats is visible on deck.

Repulse and the new battleship *Prince of Wales* were sent to the Far East in November 1941 to act as a deterrent to Japanese aggression. Immediately after their arrival, however, the Japanese attacked Pearl Harbor and invaded Hong Kong and Malaya. The two big warships attempted to intercept invasion forces crossing the South China Sea, but they were caught without air cover and sunk by Japanese land-based torpedo planes and bombers. The disaster, which signaled the decline of British power and influence in the region, also announced the end of the era of the armored ship.

Plate 51.

PRINCE OF WALES and **AUGUSTA**

Placentia Bay, Newfoundland, 1941

The battleship *Prince of Wales* enters Placentia Bay in Newfoundland carrying the British Prime Minister Winston Churchill to his rendezvous with U.S. President Franklin D. Roosevelt in August 1941. Their meeting resulted in the Atlantic Charter, forerunner of the Charter of the United Nations.

The ship on the right of the picture is the U.S. heavy-cruiser *Augusta*, which for many years served as the flagship of the Atlantic fleet. She is flying the Presidential standard from the mainmast.

The stately *Prince of Wales*, paradigm of battleships, is tall, broad in the beam, massively armed, and displays along her side the splayed top edge of her formidable armored belt.

Prominent fire-control directors are characteristic of the period; as yet radar antennae were only modest elements in a warship's silhouette. The battleship is dazzle painted and streaked with rust from her Atlantic crossing. Her signal flags depict her recognition signal, "Battleship 19," and the instruction, "Do not fire a salute."

CHAPTER XIV

BISMARCK AND PRINCE OF WALES

To the surprise of many experts, all six major naval powers found it necessary to start the construction of new battleships in the late 1930s. Notwithstanding the growing effectiveness of air power, submarines, and mines, no country could contemplate being unable to match the modern armored ships that another could put to sea.

Prince of Wales was the second ship in a class of five *King George V*-class battleships laid down in 1937. The perception of need for such ships derived from the launching of two battle cruisers, *Scharnhorst* and *Gneisenau*, in Germany; the laying of keels for two battleships of the *Bismarck* class; four battleships in Italy; and three more battleships in Japan—all in the years 1936 to 1937.

The design of the British ships was constrained by the limitations on displacement agreed originally at the Washington Conference on Naval Disarmament of 1921-22 and later extended by the London Agreement of 1934. The German ships substantially exceeded these limitations, and the Japanese ships were immensely larger.

The five *King George V*s, together with the later *Vanguard*, were the ultimate expression of British battleship design doctrine. During the planning stage there was agonizing debate on the inevitable trade-off between speed, protection, and armament. Nine 15" guns were favored for the main armament, to be arranged in the same disposition as was chosen for the *Washington*-class and subsequent American battleships. The decision was made eventually to opt for twelve 14" in three quadruple turrets, but in the end B turret had to be made a twin in order to ensure that the displacement stayed within treaty limits.

The protagonists of a more numerous battery of smaller caliber, enabling a higher rate of fire, were seemingly vindicated by the course of the final action with *Bismarck*, after her crippling by aircraft, when *King George V* and *Rodney* together smothered the powerful German ship, silencing and disabling her before she was able to inflict damage.

The secondary armament of 5.25" guns in twin turrets performed a dual-purpose role: anti-ship and anti-aircraft. In this the British ships were matched by the Americans, whereas German, Italian, and Japanese designers persisted with separate secondary and anti-aircraft armaments.

The service career of *Prince of Wales*, completed in April 1941, lasted less than nine months, the shortest of any British battleship.

Immediately after joining the fleet in May, *Prince of Wales* formed part of the force sent to intercept the *Bismarck* and cruiser *Prinz Eugen*. The British battleship was built by Cammell Laird of Birkenhead, the firm that launched *Phlegethon*, *Alabama*, and *Huascar*. Dockyard workers were still on board making adjustments to her main armament mechanisms, and her crew were learning the ropes on their new ship.

The two German raiders had set out from Norway and entered the North Atlantic between Iceland and Greenland. Their intention was to disrupt the procession of convoys that was so vital to the sustenance of Britain's war effort. The operation attempted to repeat the success of *Scharnhorst* and

Name: **PRINCE OF WALES**
Nationality: British
Builder: Cammell Laird, Birkenhead
Launched: 1939
Displacement: 38,000 tons
Length: 745 feet
Armament: Ten 14"; sixteen 5.25"; sixteen
2-pounder; rockets
Armor: Belt 15"; Deck 6"
Speed: 28 knots

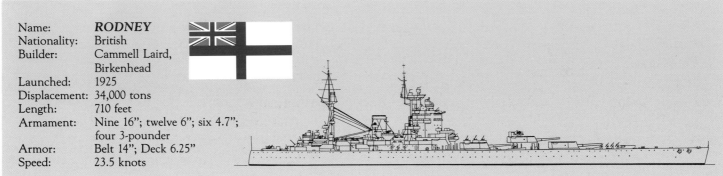

Name: **RODNEY**
Nationality: British
Builder: Cammell Laird,
Birkenhead
Launched: 1925
Displacement: 34,000 tons
Length: 710 feet
Armament: Nine 16"; twelve 6"; six 4.7";
four 3-pounder
Armor: Belt 14"; Deck 6.25"
Speed: 23.5 knots

Gneisenau, which four months earlier had followed the same route; in the course of eight weeks, the German ships had eluded action with British battleships and succeeded in sinking 22 ships. The two battle cruisers were still at Brest, and the prospect of all four warships linking up in a combined operation was alarming.

British heavy cruisers of the Northern Patrol picked up *Bismarck* and *Prinz Eugen* on their radar and shadowed them. A force under the command of Vice-Admiral Holland, consisting of the renowned but out-dated battle cruiser *Hood*, *Prince of Wales*, and six destroyers, was directed from Scapa Flow to intercept.

It was patchy, squally weather. Holland failed to cut off the enemy and was obliged to resort to a head-on approach, which allowed only his forward guns to be brought to bear. *Hood* was in the lead; although she was the weaker of his ships, she was seasoned, well-trained, and her gunnery radar was in working order. He would have been anxious to

approach quickly to within 30,000 yards, at which range the risk of plunging shellfire would be less, but to maintain a distance of 22,000 yards, within which his ship's side armor would become vulnerable to penetration.

Both sides opened fire with ranging salvos, but evidence now available indicates that the distance was already down to 18,000 yards when *Hood* was hit. She was in the act of turning to bring her full armament to bear when she was struck by a shell from *Bismarck* that caused her to blow up. Her armored belt was not deep, and the projectile probably entered just above or below it and penetrated to the cordite magazines.

Prince of Wales was only in action for 15 minutes. Despite teething troubles with radar and guns and fumbling by gun crews, which at one stage caused the jamming of all but a single 14" gun, she succeeded in scoring three hits on *Bismarck*. They were enough to bring about the German ship's eventual destruction.

Damage caused by *Prince of Wales* reduced the

battleship's speed by two knots and caused a serious oil leak. This led Admiral Lutjens to abandon his Atlantic sortie.

Prince of Wales, however, did not emerge unscathed. One hit on her bridge caused serious casualties, another disabled two of her secondary-armament directors, and a third penetrated the ship's side below the armored belt but fortunately failed to explode. It was only discovered later.

With her main armament temporarily incapacitated, *Prince of Wales* turned away and broke off the action. *Bismarck* and *Prinz Eugen* made their escape. For days the German ships were lost in the murky weather. *Bismarck* was spotted once and attacked by carrier-borne torpedo aircraft. Then she was lost again until, amidst heightening anxiety, she was located by aerial reconnaissance. This time carrier planes succeeded in winging her; a torpedo hit on the stern caused the rudder to jam. Unable to escape, the mighty ship wallowed in the ocean swell while her pursuers converged. Destroyers made a night attack, and at dawn on May 26, three days after the first interception, the battleships *King George V* and *Rodney* came upon the formidable raider.

It must have been in everyone's mind that *Bismarck* could well have destroyed her new attackers, just as she had so devastatingly proven herself capable of doing. Unable to maneuver, however, she was now at a disadvantage, and within ten minutes *Bismarck* was hit several times, and her own fire slackened. Within half an hour her main armament was silenced, her communications and fire-control systems were destroyed, and most of her senior officers were killed by a hit on the foretop.

King George V, in the same way as her sister ship, suffered mechanical breakdowns in her main armament, but neither British ship was damaged. They continued to pound the German battleship for 30 minutes before being obliged to break off the action

for shortage of fuel. The heroic German crew fought on in hopeless conditions, just as their colleagues had in von Spee's armored cruisers when caught by Sturdee in December 1914. Finally torpedoes were fired to make the wrecked battleship sink; they were assisted by scuttling charges laid by *Bismarck*'s own crew. As in the case of *Hood*, almost the entire crew went down with the ship.

King George V and *Prince of Wales* were ready only in the nick of time to pit against the new German battleships. *Scharnhorst*, *Gneisenau*, *Bismarck*, and *Tirpitz* were capable of outstripping all other British capital ships except the three elderly battle cruisers, and these latter ships were vulnerable in the face of enemy heavy ships. The third ship of the *King George V* class, *Duke of York*, eventually accomplished the destruction of *Scharnhorst*. The German ship was surprised one night in December 1943 off the North Cape of Norway, after attempting an attack on one of the convoys to Russia. This time the British gunnery was reliable and accurate. *Scharnhorst* was badly damaged, brought to a halt by destroyer attacks, and finally destroyed by gunfire and torpedoes.

Bismarck's sister ship *Tirpitz* had a less adventurous career. In January 1942 she was sent to Norway, where for more than two years she remained a threat to the northern convoys. Allied war supplies destined for Russia had to thread a narrow passage between Arctic pack ice and the northwest coast of Norway to Murmansk.

During her first operation in March 1942, she was attacked by 12 Albacore torpedo bombers from the carrier *Victorious*, but she managed to evade all torpedoes. The opportunity never recurred, for the battleship spent the rest of her life in the confined waters of fjords where the launching of torpedoes from aircraft was impracticable.

The mere absence of *Tirpitz* from her base at

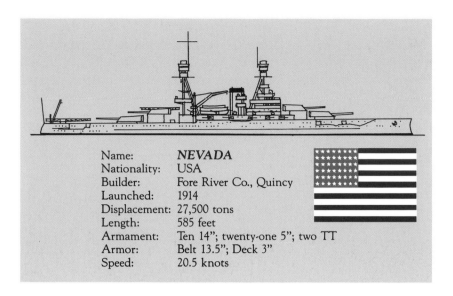

Name:	**NEVADA**
Nationality:	USA
Builder:	Fore River Co., Quincy
Launched:	1914
Displacement:	27,500 tons
Length:	585 feet
Armament:	Ten 14"; twenty-one 5"; two TT
Armor:	Belt 13.5"; Deck 3"
Speed:	20.5 knots

Faettenfjord near Trondheim, reported by aerial reconnaissance, was enough to cause the British to order the dispersal of one big convoy. The consequences were disastrous, for the scattered merchant ships were massacred by German submarines and aircraft. When *Tirpitz* was joined in Altenfjord by *Scharnhorst* and *Lützow* in March 1943, convoys to Russia were suspended entirely for five months.

Two attempts to sink her were unsuccessful. The first attack by midget submarines occurred when she lay in Kaafjord on September 22, 1943. The battleship was badly damaged by mines that were laid beneath her hull. One of the submarines was forced to surface, and the crew was captured before the time-fused charges had gone off. Alerted to the danger, *Tirpitz* was hauled out of the way in time to avoid the worst effects of the underwater explosions.

Repair work after the first attack was almost complete when the battleship was the target of a raid by carrier-borne aircraft from *Victorious* and *Furious* on April 3, 1944. The battleship lay in Altenfjord and was attacked by 40 Barracuda aircraft, which achieved 14 direct hits with bombs. The damage was crippling,

but the ship remained afloat, and the British were not to know how badly she was hurt.

Finally, in November 1944 an attack by 36 Lancaster heavy bombers dropping 1,200-pound bombs from high altitude succeeded in penetrating both armored decks and caused *Tirpitz* to capsize.

It is an interesting question whether the Royal Navy would not have been better advised to devote more resources to aircraft-carrier construction and less to battleships in the 1930s. Aircraft were essential in locating commerce raiders, and torpedo attack by carrier-borne planes played a vital role in slowing *Bismarck*. It should be borne in mind, however, that carrier-borne planes of the era were slow and primitive compared to those of later war years. Aircraft operations were extremely dependent on weather conditions; airborne torpedo attack against well-armed ships at sea was a shaky business, and a single hit might not be enough. In short, the technique was as yet uncertain, and a nation dependent on the sea could not rely on air power to conclusively stop an enemy raider.

Winston Churchill was deeply impressed by the threat represented by German capital ships, and conscious of the strain put upon British resources in 1941 by the presence of *Bismarck* in Norway and *Scharnhorst* and *Gneisenau* at Brest. These heavy units comprised a textbook example of the Fleet in Being as described by Captain Mahan. Their existence and their state of readiness were a relentless source of anxiety to the British, requiring superior numbers of ships to be constantly available and necessitating endless surveillance of the enemy ports.

Dutch, French, and British possessions in the Far East lay defenseless while battle rolled on in Europe. With Russia fighting desperately to resist being overwhelmed by the German war machine, Japan recognized this as her opportunity to expunge the presence of European powers in the East.

Plate 52.

NEVADA and CALIFORNIA

Pearl Harbor, 1941

Twice before, Japan had launched a preemptive attack on her enemy: once in 1894 against China and again in 1904 against Russia at Port Arthur. On Sunday morning December 7, 1941, Japan struck again by sending a total of 355 carrier-borne aircraft against the American naval base at Oahu in the Hawaiian Islands.

Surprise was complete, and the results at first seemed appalling. All eight active battleships in Pearl Harbor were sunk or damaged, together with a target battleship, three cruisers, and other smaller ships.

The catastrophe masked the vital fact that not a single American aircraft carrier had been present. The seven unscathed carriers became by default the principal arm of the U.S. fleet, and three of them broke the sharp edge of Japanese naval air power at the Battle of Midway six months later.

Nevada, on the left, was the only battleship present that was able to get under way during the initial Japanese raid. She became the prime target of the second wave of air-

craft, and badly damaged, she was beached to prevent her sinking in the fairway. Later repaired and modernized, she rejoined the fleet early in 1943.

California was more seriously damaged, and only heroic efforts by her crew prevented the ship from capsizing. She was raised and reconstructed but did not get back into service until 1944.

None could have anticipated quite how high-flown were Japanese imperial ambitions, no more than foreigners had been allowed to learn the true dimensions and seriousness of her naval preparations.

Nevertheless, by November 1941 there were indications. The Japanese invaded French Indo-China, and Britain decided that it was necessary to dispatch a powerful squadron to Singapore as an earnest of her resolution. Churchill, in particular, considered that the arrival of major naval units would have a sobering effect.

There were no illusions in London that two capital ships alone could supply an adequate defense, any more than at this stage in the war it was supposed that ships could operate without air cover. The modern armored-deck aircraft carrier *Indomitable* was to have formed part of the squadron, but when she was damaged by grounding at Jamaica in November, the rest of the force sailed without her. It was composed of *Prince of Wales* and the battle cruiser *Repulse*, 25 years old but recently modernized, plus four accompanying destroyers. The force made its way around the Cape and via Mombasa with maximum publicity. The objective was deterrence.

Five days after the two armored ships arrived at Singapore, the Japanese launched their unannounced attack on Pearl Harbor and simultaneosly invaded Siam, Malaya, and Hong Kong.

Admiral Phillips sailed to attack the Japanese, who had landed on the northern part of the east coast of Malaya. The British ships were spotted from the air and sensibly abandoned their original intention. They then diverted to investigate a second reported invasion nearer Singapore. Sighted by submarine, the following morning they were attacked from the air by a massive force of 85 bombers and torpedo-carrying aircraft. The aircraft were based around Saigon in French Indo-China.

The plane crews were highly trained in this kind of operation, having carried out annual exercises with their fleet, and since September of that year they had practiced launching unarmed torpedoes set to run deep under friendly ships. Japanese surface forces consisting of numerous cruisers and destroyers were in the vicinity, as well as a strong force of ten submarines and a mine-laying group, but the responsibility for attacking the British force was placed in the hands of aircrews.

The British ships were within range of fighter escort from the mainland, and arrangements had been made for air cover to be provided. When the need arose, however, the airfields had been overrun by the enemy and aerial protection was no longer available.

Prince of Wales and *Repulse* were subjected to six attacks over a period of an hour. The first was by high-level bombers directed against *Repulse*. One hit was scored, which did not penetrate the armored deck and did little damage. One aircraft was shot down. The second attack was by torpedo bombers; *Repulse* was unscathed, but *Prince of Wales* was struck by two torpedoes, one of them in the stern, just as in the case of *Bismarck*. The ensuing explosion buckled the port outer propeller shaft, which continued to revolve, causing disastrous damage in a whole series of compartments along that side of the ship. Speed was reduced to 15 knots, and the ship would no longer answer the helm. The third attack was directed against *Repulse*, but again she managed to twist and turn at high speed, combing the tracks of the underwater missiles.

The fourth attack was conclusive. The 26 Bettys of Kanoya Air Corps were the elite of the Japanese Navy's long-range torpedo bombers. They closed in to within 1,000 yards of their targets at an altitude of 100 to 150 feet above the sea before launching. Four hits were obtained on the starboard side of *Prince of Wales*. *Repulse* was unable to evade simultaneous attacks from both sides, and as a result she suffered five torpedo hits. The battle cruiser shot down two aircraft of this wave.

The fifth wave of Japanese aircraft failed to find the main target, and expended their bombs without effect on the British destroyers. The sixth and final attack by high-level bombers took place after *Repulse* had capsized, and it was directed at the crippled *Prince of Wales*. One bomb hit the ship without penetrating the armored deck, but near-misses may have added to the underwater damage aft. Twenty minutes later the battleship rolled over and sank. Most of the crew of both ships were rescued from the water.

The effect of this calamity was shattering. It was not so much the bold demonstration of air power that seemed at the time such a revolutionary experience. It was the strategic and political consequences that reverberated around the world. That Japan should have been capable of creating and training so deadly a force able to strike simultaneously at Pearl Harbor and in the Gulf of Siam was a shock to the West. That the myth of European superiority could be so rudely stripped bare caused a drastic political reappraisal in Southeast Asia.

In strategic terms the loss of the squadron left little to protect Singapore. Its defense in prewar plans had rested on Britain's ability to dispatch the main fleet from the Mediterranean, accompanied by a substantial force of modern aircraft. Such forces did not now exist.

British troops were rushed in from India, but they served only to swell the number of prisoners-of-war taken by the Japanese when the island inevitably fell. A token Allied force of cruisers was destroyed in the Battle of the Java Sea, and there was nothing left to prevent the Japanese Navy from establishing control over the Indian Ocean if it chose to do so.

In political terms the sinking of two ships brought an end to nearly 200 years of British supremacy in

the region. Loss of confidence in the established order aroused new aspirations, stimulated new initiatives. No doubt the time was ripe in any case, but there would be no going back to the old order after the war. The current renaissance of the region, epitomized by the amazing virility of Singapore, seems to have been sparked by the events of December 1941.

Britain was the predominant naval power throughout the era of the armored ship. She was dependent as no other nation on seaborne commerce for survival and was obliged, therefore, to deploy the means to protect it. At the same time her political power flowed from maintenance of the foremost worldwide navy. It speaks of this relationship that her decline as a world power was signaled by the sinking of her newest battleship.

CHAPTER XV

THE LAST ENCOUNTERS

Japan had ceased to order her navy ships from foreign yards and had already built Dreadnoughts of her own, when she decided in 1910 to place an order with Vickers for her first battle cruiser. *Kongo* was designed by Sir David Thurston, and completed at Barrow-in-Furness in 1913. Three sister ships were built in Japan, and their construction commenced as soon as blueprints were available, long before delivery of the prototype.

Kongo could be described as the first fast battleship. Not only was her main armament of slightly heavier caliber and better disposed than that in the British *Lion*-class battle cruisers, but her protection was considerably more comprehensive, and her secondary battery of 6" guns was equal to that of a battleship. The Admiralty was so impressed that the design of *Tiger*, the fourth unit of the *Lion* class, was modified along similar lines. As late as 1917 Admiral Jellicoe recommended that an approach be made for the purchase of the four *Kongo*-class ships from Japan.

Throughout their long period of service, the *Kongos* were highly regarded, and because of treaty limitations on the construction of new ships, they were the subject of two major reconstructions. After the first, in the late 1920s, they were reclassified as battleships. During the 1930s they were again rebuilt; this time they were given new propulsion machinery of twice the power. Their speed was raised to 30 knots, higher than originally designed, to allow them to operate with carriers.

All but one of the Japanese heavy ships were sunk by the end of the Second World War, the majority of them by air attack or by submarine. There were only two occasions when Japanese and American battleships engaged one another in action, and these instances were the last encounters ever to occur between armored ships. *Kirishima*, one of *Kongo*'s sister ships, took part in the first of these.

The naval battle of Guadalcanal in the Solomon Islands took place in two phases. On the night of November 12, 1942, the Japanese planned a bombardment preparatory to landing massive reinforcements for the beleaguered garrison. The fleet included *Kirishima* and her sister ship *Hiei*. They ran into an American force in the darkness, and in the ensuing mêlée the American cruisers and destroyers were very badly mauled. *Hiei*, nevertheless, was severely damaged by 8" armor-piercing shells at close range, and next morning she was unable to escape destruction at the hands of bombers and torpedo planes based on the island. The failure of the Japanese to destroy the airfield proved costly.

In spite of this setback, the Japanese persisted with their intentions. Four heavy cruisers were sent in the next night to bombard Henderson Field, and troop transports pressed on under destroyer escort to make their landings at Tassafaronga on the following day. American aircraft were still able to operate out of Guadalcanal, however; they sank one of the heavy cruisers and damaged another. Together with Flying Fortresses from Espiritu Santo and planes from the approaching carrier *Enterprise*, they carried out successive attacks on the merchant ships, sinking seven out of eleven before they reached the island.

The second phase of the battle took place on the night of November 14, when Admiral Kincaid's task force, including *Enterprise* and the new battleships *Washington* and *South Dakota*, arrived off Guadalcanal.

Plate 53.

VITTORIO VENETO

Near Cape Matapan, Eastern Mediterranean, 1941

During the German invasion of Greece in 1941, the British shipped forces from the Middle East in a vain attempt to help their ally, but the Italian navy intervened. In this picture the Italian battleship *Vittorio Veneto*, being attacked by Fairey Albacore aircraft from the carrier *Formidable*, is retiring westward at her full speed of 31 knots, all anti-aircraft guns in action.

One of the British planes was successful, and the damage caused by her torpedo slowed the battleship to 8 knots. *Vittorio Veneto* was gradually able to work back up again to 19 knots, and with the coming of darkness, she made good her escape.

The three Italian heavy cruisers accompanying the battleship were not so fortunate. One was stopped by an aerial torpedo, and then all three were caught in the night by the main force of the British fleet. None of the Italian cruisers survived.

Victorio Veneto was one of a class of four powerful battleships laid down from 1934 to 1940. The first two were intended as counters to the French *Dunkerque* and *Strasbourg*, but the Italian construction program in turn gave rise to the four projected French battleships of the *Richelieu* class. Only three *Venetos* and two *Richelieus* were ever completed.

Name: *VITTORIO VENETO*
Nationality: Italian
Builder: CRA, Trieste
Launched: 1937
Displacement: 43,377 tons
Length: 779 feet
Armament: Nine 15"; twelve 6"; four 4.7"; twelve 3.5"
Armor: Belt 13.75"; Deck 8"
Speed: 31.5 knots

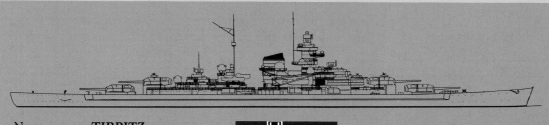

Name: *TIRPITZ*
Nationality: German
Builder: Wilhelmshaven Navy Yard
Launched: 1939
Displacement: 45,226 tons
Length: 824 feet
Armament: Eight 15"; twelve 5.9"; sixteen 4.1"
Armor: Belt 12.5"; Deck 4.75"
Speed: 30 knots

Plate 54.

TIRPITZ

Sognefjord, Norway, 1942

In January 1942 the handsome battleship *Tirpitz* entered Sognefjord on her way to northern Norway. The rest of her operational career was spent in the far north. She made few sorties, but for nearly three years she remained a constant source of anxiety in case she should emerge and fall upon the British convoys taking war supplies to Russia.

Two attempts to sink her in the fjords succeeded only in causing damage. *Tirpitz* was eventually destroyed in November 1944 by heavy bombs dropped from high-altitude bombers.

Features of interest in the painting are one of the ship's Arado Ar 196 float planes preceding *Tirpitz* up the fjord to look for lurking submarines and the Type 43 minesweeper moving close inshore to starboard.

Tirpitz carries an impressive array of radar and radio aerials, and her fire-control directors and searchlights are protected by hemispherical hoods. The two large cranes, which are seen elevated to 45 degrees, were used for hoisting float planes out of the water after landing, as well as for the handling of the ships' boats. The decks are coated with ice, and crew members on deck are wearing greatcoats.

Name:	**MISSOURI**
Nationality:	USA
Builder:	New York Navy Yard
Launched:	1942
Displacement:	49,560 tons
Length:	887 feet
Armament:	Nine 16"; twenty 5"
Armor:	Belt 12.25"; Deck 6"
Speed:	33 knots

They had been ordered up at full speed from Noumea in New Caledonia, the location of Admiral Halsey's headquarters to the southeast of the Solomons.

Japanese forces had been regrouped under the command of Admiral Kondo for a second attempt to destroy the U.S. Marines' air base on Guadalcanal. They comprised *Kirishima*, two heavy cruisers, two light cruisers, and eight destroyers.

The Americans had been warned of the approach of this force by the submarine *Trout*; Kincaid withdrew his carrier and sent Admiral Lee with the battleships to patrol. Only the American ships were equipped with radar, but the first contact was made by lookouts on the leading Japanese cruiser. Unwittingly, Admiral Lee turned across the path of the Japanese columns, and in the darkness the lines raced passed one another with a bewildering exchange of gunfire and torpedoes.

The leading American destroyers were caught unawares, and two of them were sunk. As the U.S. battleships came into action, a Japanese destroyer received the brunt of their fire, following which the third and fourth American destroyers were disabled.

Bearing down in the darkness was the last of Kondo's columns, consisting of the battleship, two heavy cruisers, and two destroyers. At this critical moment something tripped out in *South Dakota's* electrical system, causing the loss of her gunnery-control radar and also apparently silencing her guns. Furthermore, the two American battleships were not in line, having been obliged to take evasive action to avoid collision with damaged destroyers.

When *Kirishima* suddenly made her presence known by illuminating *South Dakota* with searchlights, *Washington* was masked to view to the south. The hapless *South Dakota* was smothered by fire from all five Japanese ships. Fortunately for her, the Japanese were loaded with bombardment ammunition, not armor-piercing shell, and the Americans sustained no vital injury to the ship.

Until *Kirishima's* searchlights lit up *South Dakota*, the radar operators in *Washington* had been unable to distinguish which of the battleships visible on the screen was friend and which was foe. Once enlightened, the second American battleship exacted a terrible revenge on the Japanese. *Kirishima* was hit by nine 16" rounds. Her rudder jammed, making her helpless, and Kondo finally ordered her abandonment as he retired with the remainder of his force.

The last time that battleships engaged one another was at the Battle of Surigao in the Philippines in the small hours of October 25, 1944.

When the Americans massed to recapture the Philippine Islands, the Japanese determined to make one last desperate attempt to reverse the course of the war. The Battle of Leyte Gulf was the largest sea battle of the war, and it brought about the demise of the Imperial Japanese Navy.

Four distinct Japanese forces took part in an enormous concerted operation. Admiral Nishimura's was but a part. His command consisted of the reconstructed First World War battleships *Yamashiro* and *Fuso*, the new cruiser *Mogami*, and four destroyers. The role of the seven Japanese ships was to sail from Brunei in North Borneo for the island of Leyte in the center of the Philippine group, passing across the Sulu Sea and north of Mindanao to emerge at the scene of the American invasion. Other Japanese forces were to converge simultaneously, having passed through the Philippines further north. At the same time a substantial Japanese carrier force was to approach the islands from the northeast to act as a decoy. The Americans were unaware that the shortage of experienced carrier-aircraft pilots, planes, and fuel meant that this carrier force was not the threat that it appeared.

The U.S. forces were divided between Admiral Halsey's Third Fleet, with 16 carriers, six fast battleships, and overwhelming numbers of cruisers and destroyers, and the Seventh Fleet, which was to carry out the actual landings and provide close support. The latter fleet, under separate command, included six of the older but modernized battleships, and 18 small escort carriers (converted merchant ships) for air cover.

The Japanese approaching from Borneo were detected by American submarines, and the main group under Admiral Kurita was attacked by submarines and aircraft throughout October 23 and 24.

Nishimura's force escaped lightly, but a float plane that had catapulted from one of the Japanese ships reported the presence of six battleships lying in wait for them at the north end of the Straits of Surigao.

Admiral Oldendorf, in command of these American battleships, had been engaged in shore bombardment in support of the infantry landings. He decided to arrange an in-depth defense, disposing motor-torpedo boats (P.T. boats) and destroyers amongst the islands on either side of the 40-mile-long passage of the Straits. A screen of destroyers and cruisers flanked his battle line, which was placed across the northern exit.

As Nishimura's ships entered the Mindanao Sea, followed by a further three cruisers and four destroyers under Admiral Shima that had been sent south from Japan, they were attacked by the first section of P.T. boats. As the Japanese steamed steadily up the Straits by the light of a quarter moon,

they were subjected to successive attacks gallantly pressed home by torpedo-boat crews.

Japanese ships by this stage of the war possessed radar, but Oldendorf's P.T. boats lay close to either shore, where they were obliterated on the screens. As one flotilla after another launched their torpedoes from point-blank range, the Japanese suffered severely. *Fuso* was disabled and sank three hours later. Three destroyers were hit, and *Yamashiro* was struck by two torpedoes. Finally, when *Yamashiro* was 23,000 yards from the American battle line, she came under a withering fire directed by those ships with the most up-to-date radar. In 15 minutes the Japanese battleship and the cruiser *Mogami* were hit countless times, and both were set on fire. *Yamashiro* turned back, but incredibly she put up a stiff resistance to further destroyer assaults as she struggled to make her way south. She was eventually sunk by two further torpedoes.

Admiral Shima's force coming on behind blundered into the retiring remnants. The two leading Japanese cruisers turned to fire torpedoes at the enemy, but *Mogami*, ablaze and out of control, collided with Shima's flagship.

American cruisers and destroyers pursued the damaged ships, and by daylight aircraft joined in the attack. *Mogami* and another cruiser were sunk, leaving only two cruisers still afloat.

The rest of the battle was being played out far to the north. Admiral Halsey had indeed been persuaded to chase after the empty Japanese carriers. He failed to make clear to the Seventh Fleet that the Straits of San Bernardino were being left unprotected. Despite tremendous punishment from the air, in the course of which the giant new battleship *Musashi* had been sunk, the main part of the Japanese fleet under Admiral Kurita emerged into the Pacific at dawn the next day. This force included eight cruisers, eleven destroyers, and the battleships *Yamato*, *Nagato*, *Kongo*, and her sister *Haruna*.

The escort carriers of the U.S. invasion fleet lay

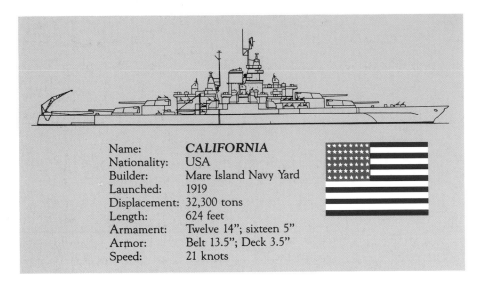

Name:	**CALIFORNIA**
Nationality:	USA
Builder:	Mare Island Navy Yard
Launched:	1919
Displacement:	32,300 tons
Length:	624 feet
Armament:	Twelve 14"; sixteen 5"
Armor:	Belt 13.5"; Deck 3.5"
Speed:	21 knots

unprotected in Kurita's path. A desperate situation called for desperate measures. American destroyers launched bold attacks against overwhelming strength, pressed home with tremendous gallantry. The tiny carriers tried to make good their escape behind smoke, aided by a heavy squall of rain. Returning aircraft were launched on attacks against the enemy.

Kurita, in his turn, was the one to be deceived. Supposing that he was being drawn towards Halsey's principal force of large fast carriers, and with a vivid recollection of the sinking of *Musashi* the previous day, he ordered his scattered ships to turn back.

The Japanese carrier force to the north was largely annihilated by Admiral Halsey, although the two hybrid battleship-carriers *Hyuga* and *Ise*, which formed part of it, managed to extricate themselves.

All the years of preparation—of building, equipping, and training a fleet—had been cast away in one mighty gamble. Suddenly, the balance of power had been tilted completely. The American victory was as sweeping as had been Japan's at the Battle of Tsushima 40 years before.

Perhaps symbolically, the Japanese surrender was signed on board a battleship. It took place on September 2, 1945, on *Missouri*. Amongst the great congregation of Allied ships in Tokyo Bay, one, *West Virginia*, had been present at Pearl Harbor, and three were sister ships of *Prince of Wales*.

Plate 55.

CALIFORNIA

Golden Gate, San Francisco, 1944

Two of the ships that were sunk at their moorings in Pearl Harbor were raised and rebuilt. One of these, *California*, only rejoined the fleet in 1944, and she had the appearance of a completely new battleship (see Plate 52 for comparison).

The other ship salvaged was *West Virginia*. She was rebuilt on similar lines, together with *California*'s sister ship *Tennessee*. *Oklahoma*, which was also sunk in shallow water, was raised but proved to be damaged beyond repair.

The rebuilt ships were given massive anti-torpedo bulges, which increased the main deck beam. The bulges were built up to upper-deck level amidships, where they provided platforms for the new 5" high-angle armament. The original 5" casemate battery disappeared in the process. The old battleships were also, of course, equipped with modern fire-control and radar technology, and they acquired a generous armament of small-caliber anti-aircraft guns on every available vantage point.

The battleship is depicted passing out to sea beneath the great span of the Golden Gate Bridge on her way to take part in the invasion of the Philippines. Her dazzle camouflage is made doubly confusing by the shadow of the bridge.

166

CHAPTER XVI
RESURRECTION

With the end of fighting in 1945, the nations concluded that whatever the pattern of future warfare, there would no longer be need for armored ships. Within four years 40 battleships had been sold out of service, and by 1960 the handful remaining had all been retired. The only exceptions were the four *Iowa*-class ships of the U.S. Navy, which were prudently wrapped in plastic and preserved in case of future need.

The U.S. battleship *New Jersey* was taken out of mothballs for use in the Korean War and later refurbished for service off the coast of Vietnam. In 1982 she became the first of the four *Iowa*-class battleships to be given an entirely new lease on life by being converted to a missile carrier. She made headlines when she appeared off the beaches of Beirut. Her sister ship *Iowa*, after similar conversion, returned to active service in 1986, and *Missouri* and *Wisconsin* have followed suit. No other steel warships ever had such a long span of useful life.

New Jersey was laid down nearly 50 years ago and completed in 1943. By 1938 international efforts to restrain the size of new warships by treaty had broken down, and the U.S. Navy was free to determine the size of its proposed new battleships to suit its needs. Limited only by the capacity of the Panama Canal locks, the new ships were designed with barely a foot of clearance on either side.

Their increased displacement compared with the *Washington* and *South Dakota* classes was devoted mainly to bigger engines and greater waterline length in order to achieve much higher speed. With unprecedented high steam pressures and nearly twice the power of the *Washingtons*, the *Iowa* class could easily maintain 33 knots at sea, well in excess of the speed of any other battleship.

The design was a well-balanced combination. Their armament of nine 16" guns was similar to their predecessors', but they were an improved model with longer barrels that conferred greater range and accuracy. Protection was enhanced by means of greater internal subdivision, particularly longitudinal bulkheads and armored decks. But in a war where their role was the support and defense of fast aircraft carriers, it was their speed that made these splendid ships so valuable.

In the era of the armored ship, there were always some who could see no virtue in moderation. Excess in any one quality of design tends to bring about weakness in another, and in all things there seems to be a law of diminishing returns. The most successful designs were balanced, so that when it came to the hazards of war, there was no one area of weakness to incapacitate the whole. In the delicate equation of armament, speed, protection, and endurance, the *Iowa* class was nicely judged, superior in every department but in no respect grotesque.

What circumstances have led to the reactivation of these fine vessels, long after it had been supposed that the era of the armored ship had come to an end?

It is certainly not as big-gun ships that the *Iowas* have been put back into service, nor is it merely a melodramatic gesture.

The battleship finally lost its importance in 1944,

Plate 56.

MUSASHI and *YAMATO*

Brunei Bay, Borneo, 1944

When news was received of American shipping gathering for the landings on Leyte Island in the Philippines, seven Japanese battleships, thirteen cruisers, and other craft were sent from Lingga Bay near Singapore to Brunei on the northwest coast of Borneo. Amongst the great gathering of warships under the grey skies, the torrential rain, and the suffocating humidity of Brunei Bay were *Musashi* and *Yamato*, the two largest armored ships ever built. From there they sailed on October 22, 1944, for the extended opera-

tion that became known as the Battle of Leyte Gulf.

The Japanese had anticipated that the giant battleships would be the decisive factor in any surface encounter with the American fleet, for their main armament of nine 18" guns had a range of more than 45,000 yards, and their shells were enormous. At the time no one outside Japan was aware of their true size.

There never came a chance to learn how accurately, how rapidly, or how reliably these great guns would perform in action. One

battleship was sunk by aircraft before the battle, and the other turned back under threat of air attack soon after the first en-counter with American surface ships. The day of the battleship was past.

craft: bombers, which comprise the prime offensive weapon; long-range fighters to protect the ship against attack by air-borne stand-off missiles; anti-submarine aircraft and helicopters; and vital air-borne early-warning aircraft to extend the scope of the ship's radar beyond the horizon. Such ships are immensely costly to build, to maintain, and to man.

Two developments have begun to increase the potential of surface warships. One is the introduction of cruise missiles, which can provide much of the same strike capability as bombers. The other is the development of comprehensive missile air defense systems like Aegis, which is capable of taking the place of fighter aircraft in the aerial defense of a fleet.

The Russians have put into service Kirov-class nuclear-powered cruisers armed with cruise missiles and with anti-aircraft missiles for defense. Their only aircraft are helicopters that are used in an anti-submarine role.

The U.S. Navy contemplated building ships of this category, too, as a way of providing part of the capabilities of the giant carriers but with much reduced manpower and cost of operation. Nevertheless, such ships would have been very expensive to build.

Thus was borne the notion of revitalizing old battleships. Their size was their most attractive feature. A Kirov carries but 20 cruise missiles, with only a fraction of the offensive power of a big American carrier, but the battleships are capable of carrying more than 300.

New Jersey operates as the nucleus of a Surface Action Group, which includes four destroyers and four frigates, some of them armed with Aegis missiles. The battleship now carries a mixture of Tomahawk cruise missiles and shorter-range Harpoon anti-ship missiles. A Surface Action Group does not have the striking power of an Aircraft Carrier Action Group, but it can fill a role in situations short of full scale war, in restricted waters, and in coastal bombardment.

when the improvement of carrier aircraft in speed, range, carrying capacity, and reliability meant that it was no longer necessary to have one big-gun ship in order to stop another. A carrier force could mount all the offensive power of a battle fleet and extend it to far greater range.

In the years following the Second World War, the most striking improvements were in the speed and capability of underwater craft. Nuclear submarines assumed the role of capital ships. Surface warships became vulnerable to more deadly types of torpedo, including one that will pass beneath the keel before exploding and thus nullify the usual means of underwater hull protection.

The United States alone has the resources to retain a force of very large aircraft carriers. With a displacement of 90,000 tons (greater than that of the liner Queen Mary), these vessels carry a force of 90 air-

The latter venue is where the big guns of the old battleships have the most obvious value. No modern weapons system can deliver such reliable and economical means of intervention. Nevertheless, it is, perhaps, their armor that is their most significant characteristic. Battleships cannot readily be injured by a surprise assault of airborne missiles, and nobody else in the world now has the capacity to fire heavy-caliber armor-piercing shells.

The earliest armored ships were used to bombard forts in the Crimea with demoralizing impunity. It should be no cause for wonder that the last remaining armored ships have returned to a corresponding role.

In spite of the enormous developments in submarines, aircraft, and missiles since 1945, surface ships are still the most explicit means of exerting leverage. In Vietnam, in the Gulf, at the Falklands, in the eastern Mediterranean, and off the coast of Nicaragua, the conspicuous presence of surface warships has been used in the grand game of power politics. A recent proposal to station an American warship off the coast of Colombia, although its purpose was only to act as a radar station for catching drug runners, aroused profound resentment in a nation that had been the victim of gunboat diplomacy in 1903.

Name:	**MUSASHI**
Nationality:	Japanese
Builder:	Kure Dockyard
Launched:	1940
Displacement:	68,010 tons
Length:	863 feet
Armament:	Nine 18.1"; twelve 6.1"; twelve 5"
Armor:	Belt 16"; Deck 9"
Speed:	27 knots

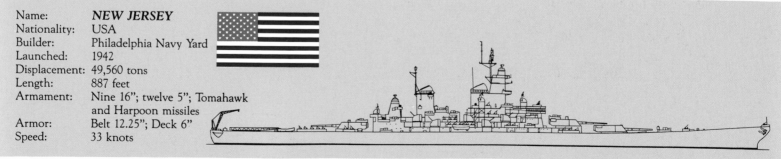

Name:	**NEW JERSEY**
Nationality:	USA
Builder:	Philadelphia Navy Yard
Launched:	1942
Displacement:	49,560 tons
Length:	887 feet
Armament:	Nine 16"; twelve 5"; Tomahawk and Harpoon missiles
Armor:	Belt 12.25"; Deck 6"
Speed:	33 knots

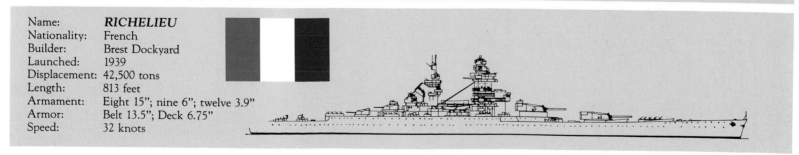

Name:	**RICHELIEU**
Nationality:	French
Builder:	Brest Dockyard
Launched:	1939
Displacement:	42,500 tons
Length:	813 feet
Armament:	Eight 15"; nine 6"; twelve 3.9"
Armor:	Belt 13.5"; Deck 6.75"
Speed:	32 knots

Plate 57.

RICHELIEU

Monte Carlo, 1954

Richelieu, one of the half-dozen battleships in the world still in commission in 1954, lies in the blue Mediterranean off the waterfront at Monte Carlo. The Sporting Club appears on the left; the Hôtel de Paris, on the right.

Note the grouping of three triple 6"-gun turrets at *Richelieu*'s stern; the main armament of eight 15" guns was all mounted on the foredeck in two quadruple turrets.

Pioneered by the French, the four-gun turret was adopted in order to reduce the length of the armored citadel and constrain the displacement of French ships. This design came at a price; a single enemy hit might eliminate half the ship's fighting power.

Richelieu was incomplete in June 1940, but she sailed under her own steam to Dakar in West Africa. There, after declining to rejoin the fight against Germany, she was attacked by the British and sustained damage by depth charges dropped from a motorboat and by a torpedo from a carrier-borne aircraft. In September 1940 she participated in the vigorous defense of Dakar, which prevented a landing by Gaullist troops, and scored a hit on the battleship *Barham* at the remarkable range of nearly 50,000 yards.

After the American landings in North West Africa, the battleship joined the Free French. *Richelieu* sailed for New York, where the damage sustained at Dakar was repaired. In 1944 she joined British carriers in operations against *Tirpitz* in Norway, and subsequently she was based at Trincomalee in Ceylon. She had a spell of duty off Indo-China before becoming a gunnery-training ship at Toulon.

Plate 58.

NEW JERSEY

Gaillard Cut, Panama Canal, 1984

In 1983 the American battleship *New Jersey* was dispatched to Lebanon, where she fired at targets on shore in December and the following January.

The reintroduction of the big gun 40 years after many thought that it had been superseded caused worldwide interest, but the recommissioning of the *Iowa*-class battleships occurred not simply for use in the fire-support role. The four ships have also been rearmed as missile carriers, mounting Tomahawk cruise missiles and Harpoon anti-

ship missiles on their superstructures.

New Jersey is seen proceeding gingerly through the Gaillard Cut, where the Panama Canal divides the hills forming the Continental Divide at Culebra. Like all American warships until the age of the supercarrier, she was designed to fit through the locks of the canal.

In this view the beautiful long, lean form of the battleship's hull can be seen to good advantage. Most battleships were broad in the beam for their length (a ratio of 1:6), but

the *Iowa* class are about 1:8.5. The length of the hull, coupled with enormous power—roughly 80 percent more than that of preceding classes—provides these ships with their impressive speed of 33 knots.

BIBLIOGRAPHY

Alden, John D. *The American Steel Navy*. Annapolis, MD: Naval Institute P, 1972.

Archibald, E.H.H. *The Fighting Ship of the Royal Navy*. Poole, Blandford P, 1984.

Attard, Joseph. *The Battle of Malta*. London: William Kimber, 1980.

Breyer, Siegfried. *Battleships of the World*. London: Conway Maritime P, 1980.

Burt, R.A., and W.C. Trotter. *Battleships of the Grand Fleet*. London: Arms & Armour P, 1982.

Campbell, N.J.M. *Battlecruisers*. London: Conway Maritime P, 1978.

Chatterton, E. Keble. *The Sea-Raiders*. London: Hurst & Blackett, 1931.

_____ . *The Königsberg Adventure*. London: Hurst & Blackett, 1932.

Childers, Erskine. *The Riddle of the Sands*. 1903. London: Penguin Books, 1952.

Critchley, Mike, ed. *The Royal Navy in Focus*. Liskeard: Maritime Books.

Corbett, Sir Julian. *History of the Great War, Naval Operations*. London: Longmans, 1920.

Elliott, Peter. *The Cross and the Ensign*. Cambridge: Patrick Stephens, 1980.

Gardiner, Robert, ed. *Camera at Sea 1939-45*. London: Conway Maritime P, 1978.

_____ , ed. *All the World's Fighting Ships 1860-1905*. London: Conway Maritime P, 1979.

_____ , ed. *All the World's Fighting Ships 1906-1921*. London: Conway Maritime P, 1985.

Gibbons, Tony. *The Complete Encyclopedia of Battleships and Battlecruisers*. London: Salamander Books, 1983.

Glover, Michael. *Waterloo to Mons*. London: Guild Publishing, 1980.

Harland, Kathleen. *The Royal Navy in Hong Kong*. Liskeard: Maritime Books.

Headrick, Daniel R. *The Tools of Empire*. New York: Oxford UP, 1981.

Holman, Gordon. *The King's Cruisers*. London: Hodder & Stoughton, 1947.

Hough, Richard. *The Potemkin Mutiny*. London: Hamish Hamilton, 1960.

_____ . *Admirals in Collision*. London: Hamish Hamilton.

_____ . *The Fleet That Had to Die*. London: Chatto & Windus, 1963.

_____ . *Dreadnought*. London: George Allen & Unwin, 1968.

_____ . *First Sea Lord*. London: George Allen & Unwin, 1969.

_____ . *The Great War at Sea*. Oxford: Oxford UP, 1983.

Howarth, David. *The Dreadnoughts*. Amsterdam: Time-Life Books, 1979.

Humble, Richard. *Battleships and Battlecruisers*. London: Winchmore, 1983.

Ireland, Bernard. *Cruisers*. London: Hamlyn, 1981.

Jane, Fred T., ed. *Fighting Ships, 1914*. London: Sampson Low, Marston, 1914.

Keegan, John. *The Price of Admiralty*. London: Hutchinson, 1988.

King, Cecil. H.M.S. *His Majesty's Ships and Their Forbears*. London: Studio Publications, 1940.

Lambert, Andrew. *Warrior*. London: Conway Maritime P, 1987.

Leather, John. *World Warships in Review 1860-1906*. London: Macdonald & Jane's, 1976.

MacDougall, Philip. *Royal Dockyards*. London: David & Charles, 1982.

Macintyre, Donald. *The Thunder of the Guns*. London: Frederick Muller, 1959.

Marder, Arthur. *The Anatomy of British Sea Power*. London: Frank Cass, 1940.

McMurtrie, Francis, ed. *Jane's Fighting Ships, 1944-45*. London: Sampson Low, Marston, 1946.

Miller, Charles. *Battle for the Bundu*. New York: Macmillan, 1974.

Morris, James. *Pax Britannica*. London: Faber & Faber, 1968.

_____ . *Heaven's Command*. London: Faber & Faber, 1973.

Padfield, Peter. *Rule Britannia*. London: Routledge & Kegan Paul, 1981.

Parkes, Oscar. *British Battleships*. London: Seeley Service, 1956.

_____ , ed. *Jane's Fighting Ships, 1931*. London: Sampson Low, Marston, 1931.

Pope, Dudley. *The Battle of the River Plate*. London: William Kimber, 1974.

Preston, Anthony, and John Batchelor. *Battleships 1856-1919*. London: Phoebus, 1977.

Raven, Alan, and John Roberts. *British Battleships of World War Two*. Annapolis, MD: Naval Institute P.

Reilly, John C., and Robert L. Scheina. *American Battleships 1886-1923*. London: Arms & Armour P, 1980.

Simpson, Colin. *The Ship that Hunted Itself*. London: Wiedenfeld & Nicholson, 1977.

Stern, Rob. *U.S. Battleships in Action*. 2 vols. Carroltown: Squadron/Signal Publications, 1984.

Sutton, Jean. *Lords of the East*. London: Conway Maritime P, 1981.

Talbot-Booth, ed. *Ships and the Sea*. London: Sampson Low, Marston, 1936.

Trotter, Wilfrid Pym. *The Royal Navy in Old Photographs*. London: J.M. Dent & Sons, 1975.

Tuchman, Barbara. *The Zimmerman Telegram*. London: Constable, 1959.

_____ . *The Guns of August*. New York: Macmillan, 1962. Co-published as *August 1914* (London: Constable, 1962.)

_____ . *The Proud Tower*. New York: Macmillan, 1966.

Van Der Vat, Dan. *The Last Corsair*. London: Hodder & Stoughton, 1983.

_____ . *The Ship That Changed the World*. London: Hodder & Stoughton, 1985.

White, Colin. *The Heyday of Steam*. Emsworth: Kenneth Mason, 1951.

Whitley, M.J. *German Cruisers of World War Two*. London: Arms & Armour P, 1985.

Wilson, Timothy. *Flags at Sea*. Her Majesty's Stationery Office, 1986.

NOTES

1. Displacement is the best measure of size of a ship; it simply means the weight of water displaced when she floats. Where possible, displacements quoted are Standard, which includes crew, guns, and ammunition but not fuel, freshwater, or stores.

2. Morris, James. *Pax Britannica*. London: Routledge & Kegan Paul, 1981.

3. Hough, Richard. *The Fleet That Had to Die*. London: Chatto & Windus, 1963.

4. Macintyre, Donald. *The Thunder of the Guns*. London: Frederick Muller, 1959.

5. Tuchman, Barbara. *The Guns of August*. Macmillan: New York, 1962.

6. Tuchman, Barbara.

STATISTICS

The specification notes that accompany the small line drawings are necessarily very abbreviated. It is impossible to give a true description of the quality or the extent of a ship's armored protection in this way, let alone of other important characteristics such as endurance or underwater protection. The armor thickness quoted is always the maximum. The abbreviation TT stands for torpedo tube. The figures cited generally refer to a ship's condition as first completed. The line drawings in some cases differ from the appearance of the ship in the year illustrated in the plate, or they represent another ship of the same class.

Excerpt from *Pax Britannica* by James Morris © 1968 reprinted with permission of Faber & Faber Ltd. Excerpt from *The Fleet That Had to Die* by Richard Hough © 1963 reprinted with permission of Chatto & Windus. Excerpt from *The Thunder of the Guns* by Donald Macintyre © 1959 reprinted with permission of Frederick Muller. Excerpts from *The Guns of August* (co-published as *August 1914*) by Barbara Tuchman © 1962 reprinted with permission of Macmillan and Constable publishers.

Recognition silhouettes for *Admiral Graf Spee*, *Arizona*, *Nevada*, *Pennsylvania*, *Phlegethon*, *Repulse*, *Triumph*, the 1941-version *Queen Elizabeth*, and *Warspite* prepared by Ian H. Marshall. All others reprinted from the *Conway's All the World's Fighting Ships* series and used with permission of Conway Maritime Press Ltd.

INDEX

(Illustrations are denoted by italicized page numbers)